NOMINATION POLITICS

NOMINATION POLITICS

Party Activists and Presidential Choice

Alan I. Abramowitz
and
Walter J. Stone

PRAEGER SPECIAL STUDIES • PRAEGER SCIENTIFIC

New York • Philadelphia • Eastbourne, UK
Toronto • Hong Kong • Tokyo • Sydney

Library of Congress Cataloging in Publication Data

Abramowitz, Alan I.
  Nomination politics.

  Bibliography: p.
  Includes index.
  1. Presidents—United States—Nomination.
I. Stone, Walter J. II. Title.
JK521.A27 1984   324.5   84-17891
ISBN 0-03-000519-1 (alk. paper)

Published in 1984 by Praeger Publishers
CBS Educational and Professional Publishing,
a Division of CBS Inc.
521 Fifth Avenue, New York, NY 10175 USA

456789 052 987654321

Printed in the United States of America
on acid-free paper

PREFACE AND
ACKNOWLEDGMENTS

This is a book about presidential nominations. Most studies
of presidential nominations in recent years have concentrated
on presidential primary elections. Since the post-1968 reforms
of the nomination process, most of the delegates to the national
party conventions have been chosen in primaries, and the results
of the primaries, especially the early ones, have generally determined the outcome of the nomination. However, this book is
concerned with a different part of the presidential nominating
process, one that has received very little attention in recent
years—the selection of national convention delegates in the
caucus-convention states. In 1980, about 30 percent of the
delegates to the Democratic and Republican national conventions
were chosen through the caucus-convention process, but we
believe that the importance of this process is greater than the
number of delegates chosen in these states would indicate. The
caucus-convention states provide an opportunity to examine the
role of party activists in presidential nominating politics in states
with different political cultures and traditions. This investigation should advance our knowledge about the characteristics,
motivations, and political beliefs of party activists in the United
States.

In addition to providing an opportunity to study contemporary party activists, the caucus-convention states are interesting for another reason. Since 1980 the Democratic Party has
made significant changes in the rules governing its presidential
nominating process. As a result of the recommendations of the
Hunt Commission, elected and party officials were given a larger
role in the nomination of the 1984 Democratic presidential candidate. In addition, for the first time since 1968, there has been
a decrease in the number of states holding primary elections and
an increase in the number of states selecting delegates to the
Democratic national convention through caucus-convention procedures. It now appears that almost two-fifths of the delegates to
the 1984 Democratic national convention will be chosen in 24
states using caucus-convention procedures. Ironically, the
Republican Party, which reformed its rules and procedures
much less drastically than the Democrats after 1968, will select
almost 80 percent of its national convention delegates in primary
elections in 1984.

Whether the changes made by the Democrats for 1984 will have any long-term consequences will probably depend on the outcomes of the nominating process and the general election. If the reforms are judged successful by party leaders, there may be further efforts to expand the role of party and elected officials in the nominating process, and more states may adopt caucus-convention procedures in place of presidential primaries. Under such circumstances, it would not be surprising if the Republican Party adopted similar changes in its nominating rules and procedures. Although a return to the "brokered convention" era is very unlikely and primary elections will continue to play a major role in the nomination of presidential candidates, the sorts of party activists examined in this book may exert greater influence on presidential nominations in the future.

Many persons have provided assistance in the preparation of this book. We are grateful to our colleagues at the University of Colorado and the State University of New York at Stony Brook whose comments and suggestions helped us to clarify our thinking about presidential nominating politics as well as our writing. We are also grateful to the secretarial staff at each school, and especially to Laura King and Marilyn Ellis of the University of Colorado and Estelle Krieger of the State University of New York at Stony Brook, who each typed several chapters of the manuscript. Charles N. Brasher at the University of Colorado was extremely helpful in conducting the data analyses for Chapters 5 and 6.

We owe a special debt of gratitude to our colleagues around the country who assisted us in gathering the data on which this book is based. The collection of the data in each of the 11 caucus-convention states included in the study was performed by a team of political scientists assisted, in many states, by graduate and undergraduate students, and occasionally, by friends and family members. The political scientists who participated in the data collection were, in alphabetical order, Tod Baker, Robert Benedict, Jeffrey Brudney, John Francis, Charles Hauss, Mary Kweit, Robert Kweit, Louis Maisel, Jean McDonald, John McGlennon, Laurence Moreland, Ronald Pynn, Ronald Rapoport, Thomas Sanders, Thomas Simmons, Robert Steed, and Mary Thornberry. Without their efforts, this book would not have been possible.

Many of the political scientists who participated in the data collection also attended two conferences in Williamsburg, Virginia, at which plans were made for the study and papers were presented analyzing the data that had been gathered. Many of our own ideas were shaped by the discussions which took place

at these conferences. John McGlennon and Ronald Rapoport
of the College of William and Mary played key roles in the
organization of these conferences. We are grateful to the
National Science Foundation, which provided funding for the
two conferences in Williamsburg, and especially to Gerald Wright,
the Political Science Program Director at N.S.F., whose assistance was invaluable before, during, and after the conferences.
Finally, we owe a very large debt of gratitude to David Reed
of the College of William and Mary for his many hours of assistance in merging the data from 11 separate state surveys into
a single, usable file.

This book is dedicated to Ann and Ann.

CONTENTS

LIST OF TABLES AND FIGURES

NOMINATION POLITICS

1

INTRODUCTION: PARTY ACTIVISTS
IN PRESIDENTIAL POLITICS

Presidential elections have attracted a tremendous amount
of attention from political scientists. The reasons for this interest are not very different from those that explain the interest
of journalists, politicians, and citizens. The importance of the
office of the president, and the fact that presidential elections
serve as a barometer of the national mood explains the interest
of close observers of American politics. Presidential elections
sometimes offer a clear choice between the policy proposals of
candidates and parties, and they always hold the possibility of
important new directions in national politics. Some elections
are understood as "realigning" or "critical" because they help
to signal new electoral coalitions supporting the parties or
because they define a new public philosophy, or both. Through
careful survey research on voting in presidential elections, we
have come to learn a great deal about how citizens express their
preferences and participate in democratic politics.

Given the importance of presidential elections, it is perhaps
curious that political scientists have devoted far more effort to
understanding the general election, in which citizens choose
between the nominees of the major political parties, than they
have to comprehending the nomination process within each party
whereby the nominees are selected. Certainly a number of
excellent studies of the latter problem have been conducted,
but the discipline has generally been preoccupied with the
general election stage. We seek in this book to contribute to
our understanding of nomination politics. In particular, we are
concerned with the way presidential activists—those who become
relatively intensely involved in their party's selection of a
presidential nominee—choose to support a candidate.

The nomination process is of interest because through it
the agenda is set for the general election. By nominating

1

Hubert Humphrey in 1968, George McGovern in 1972, and Jimmy Carter in 1976 and 1980, the Democrats chose very different kinds of candidates with important consequences for the choices voters had in each election. Indeed, control over the major party nominations may be more important than control over the general election choice, precisely because of the agenda setting function of the nomination phase. Just as important, nomination campaigns may reflect important changes in the character of our politics. The nominees of the Democratic Party from 1968 through 1980 may exemplify this kind of change, and, as we shall see, most of the literature on nominations has focused upon the potential for change.

The selection of nominees to represent the parties in the general election is also of interest because it is an important example of coalition building in a sequential process of decision making. Participants may not only think about their preferences in the immediate arena (the nomination contest), but they may also anticipate the effects of their choice on the next stage (the general election). The process of choosing which candidate coalition to join in a sequential process such as this is likely to be influenced by anticipation of the next stage. A better understanding of this sequential choice may help us understand other choices such as those that go on in congressional committees as they anticipate other coalitions' interests on the floor or in the other chamber, in bureaucratic agencies as they jockey for executive and congressional support, and even in judicial decisions as they anticipate appeal or implementation elsewhere in the process. Indeed, it is difficult to think of a significant political decision that does not have some sequential quality. Even the general election choosing a president may be thought of in this way, although most citizens probably think of their choice as "final." Nonetheless, nomination choices are difficult to think of as other than part of a sequence, and an important sequence at that. Their importance in their own right, as well as possible examples of a more general phenomenon, justifies more effort in coming to understand them.

TWO MODELS OF THE PRESIDENTIAL ACTIVIST

The Purist Model

The largest proportion of research on the nomination process has come in the last decade. It was stimulated in part by a reform movement within the Democratic Party which sought to "democratize" the way in which candidates were nominated by the party. A series of reforms in the rules of the Democratic Party followed the 1968 election and were in place by the time the 1972 nomination campaign began (Crotty 1977; Polsby and Wildavsky 1980; Ceaser 1982; Polsby 1983). These reforms opened the process to wider participation by requiring local party leaders to make public the times and places of caucuses that began the process of selecting delegates to the national convention. The reforms also adopted a model of representation for the national convention that asserted the right of previously underrepresented groups within the party (explicitly women, blacks, and young people) to seats at the convention. The resulting "quota" system encouraged local leaders to seek out members of these groups for participation in the early stages of the process in order to avoid the possibility of their delegations being denied their credentials at the convention. Many states responded to these reforms by carrying the movement toward intraparty democracy to its logical conclusion and instituting presidential primaries in place of the previously favored caucus-convention system. Delegates selected in primary states could hardly be challenged at the convention on the grounds that their state's process was not open or democratic.

Following the methodological precedents set by their colleagues who had studied voters in general elections, many political scientists conducted careful surveys of participants in the postreform presidential nomination process (Kirkpatrick 1976; Soule and Clarke 1970, 1971; Hitlin and Jackson 1977; Roback 1980). These studies built almost without exception upon the earlier work of James Q. Wilson (1962) and Aaron Wildavsky (1965) in approaching the problem of how participants got involved in the process and, once involved, how they made their choice.

Wilson's concept of the "amateur" party activist has been seminal in later thinking about presidential activists. In his comparative analysis of party activists in New York, Chicago, and Los Angeles, Wilson (1962, p. 3) summarized what he meant by the concept:

An amateur is one who finds politics intrinsically interesting because it expresses a conception of the public interest. The amateur politician sees the political world more in terms of ideas and principles than in terms of persons. Politics is the determination of public policy, and public policy ought to be set deliberately rather than as the accidental

> by-product of a struggle for personal and party
> advantage. Issues ought to be settled on their
> merits; compromises by which one issue is settled
> other than on its merits are sometimes necessary,
> but they are never desirable.

In contrast, "professionals" are "preoccupied with the outcome
of politics in terms of winning or losing" (Wilson 1962, p. 4).
Wilson explicitly separates his concept from attitudes toward
reform per se and from the amount of experience or skill in
politics the party activist may have, although others have
invested his concept with this meaning.

Wilson's was not a study of presidential politics, but the
concepts "amateur" and "professional" provided nearly ready-
made answers to how activists in presidential nomination campaigns might decide whom to support for the nomination.
Amateurs could be expected to select the candidate who best
represents their issue interests. In contrast to professionals,
they would be less interested in supporting a candidate who
accommodates conflicting views by compromising or watering
down his own positions, and they would be less concerned
about the consequences, for the party organization, of their
supporting a candidate. The candidacy of Barry Goldwater
for the Republican nomination in 1964 and those of Eugene
McCarthy and George McGovern on the Democratic side in 1968
and 1972 were generally linked to amateur support. These
candidates were attractive because they were not afraid to
express their (sometimes unpopular) views. They drew their
support largely from activists who agreed with their policy
views and who felt their style was an appropriate change from
the accommodationist politics of most previous candidates.
Many of these amateur activists were relatively new to political
activism, in part because they were profoundly cynical about
"politics as usual" before their candidate's appearance on the
presidential scene. Certainly it could be said they were more
likely to be drawn into the process out of concern for the issues
than because of an interest in material rewards or party loyalty.

Aaron Wildavsky, in a study of the Goldwater delegates
to the GOP national convention in 1964, applied many of the
same kinds of distinctions Wilson had made to presidential
activists. Wildavsky (1965, p. 393) distinguished between
"purist" delegates (most of whom preferred Goldwater) and
"politicians." An important reason for supporting Goldwater,
to the purists, was the candidate's "consistency, honesty,
integrity, and willingness to stick by principles." Wildavsky

(1965, p. 394) reports an exchange between an interviewer
and a delegate that captures much of the purist mentality:

> Interviewer: What qualities should a presidential
>   candidate have?
> Delegate: Moral integrity.
> Interviewer: Should he be able to win the election?
> Delegate: No, principles are more important. I
>   would rather be one against 20,000 and believe
>   I was right. That's what I admire about Gold-
>   water. He's like that.

Purists, like amateurs, could be expected to support candidates with whom they agreed on the major issues and candidates
whose style is congenial to their perception of the appropriate
way to conduct a campaign. In his widely noted work on presidential elections with Nelson Polsby, Wildavsky defines purists
in a way that clearly states this expectation about their candidate
choice behavior (Polsby and Wildavsky 1980, pp. 22-23): "Purists
wish their views to be put forth by the parties without equivoca-
tion or compromise and although they otherwise seek to win
elections, they do not care to do this at the expense of self
expression. . . . In the purist conception of things, instead
of a party convention being a place where a party meets to
choose candidates who can win elections by pleasing voters, it
becomes a site for finding a candidate who will embody the
message delegates seek to express."

We refer to the Wilson and Polsby-Wildavsky characterization
of the amateur-purist as the "purist model," and we use the
terms "amateur" and "purist" interchangeably. Because this
is a book about activists' candidate choice, we are most interested
in the purist model's predictions about candidate choice. The
discussion above clearly suggests that to the extent activists
adopt the purist style, they will choose candidates who express
their issue and ideological preferences, even if that means they
must support a candidate for the nomination who is less likely
to win the November election than one of his opponents for the
party's nomination. The model suggests that the sequential
character of the presidential selection process will be of no
concern to purists in supporting a candidate for the nomination
except to assure that the party's nominee will express their
views during the general election campaign.

The purist model has come to dominate most of the survey
research done on presidential activists. Researchers armed
with questions designed to tap various aspects of the purist

style (including the orientation of activists toward winning and compromise) have conducted numerous studies of national party convention delegates in the years since Wildavsky's study of the Goldwater delegates. Much of this work has been motivated by a concern with change reflected in (and possibly caused by) reforms of the nomination process. Beginning with the civil rights movement of the 1960s, and continuing with the Vietnam and social issues of the late 1960s and 1970s, active participants in nomination politics seemed to be motivated by deeply held issue opinions. And using questionnaire items suggested by the purist model, researchers found evidence that these issue concerns increasingly were reflected in nomination politics by activists of a purist stripe. Jeane Kirkpatrick (1976) concluded from her extensive study of 1972 delegates that a new breed of activists, encouraged by the reforms of the process and by candidates with styles congenial to their own, were participating at higher rates than ever before. Ladd and Hadley (1978, pp. 333-42) suggest that the GOP nomination of Goldwater and the Democratic Party's nomination of McGovern were harbingers of a fundamental change toward increased concern with issues and increased influence of "issue activists" in presidential politics. Soule and McGrath (1975, p. 511) were able to show from a comparative analysis of data from the 1968 and the (post-reform) 1972 Democratic nominating conventions that the proportion of amateurs attending more than doubled from 23 to 51 percent.

The Rational Choice Model of the Presidential Activist

Despite the nearly unanimous acceptance of the purist model in the literature based upon surveys of contemporary presidential activists, there are good theoretical reasons to suggest activists will not merely select candidates on the basis of ideological positions or style. By and large, presidential activists are well educated and sophisticated about politics, even if they are sometimes new to the presidential arena. Given their sophistication, how likely is it that they will ignore the general election phase when choosing from among contenders for their party's nomination? To do so might amount to making a decision to help the opposite party to the White House. If activists support candidates solely upon ideological or issue preferences, they run the risk of choosing a candidate who will prove to be extremely weak against the opposite party's nominee, thus conceding the general election. Capturing a major party nomination with little or no chance to win the general election amounts to winning a prize of dubious value. Activists (and candidates) who invest an incredible amount of energy in nomination campaigns would seem to be likely to want to win, as well as to want to promote a particular ideology.

That activists may wish to associate themselves with a winner does not mean they will never miscalculate. Supporters of Barry Goldwater in 1964 may have been attracted to their candidate's thesis that there was a "hidden majority" of conservative voters who were waiting for the Republicans to nominate a true-blue conservative before they would vote overwhelmingly for the GOP, thus creating a majority for Goldwater (Converse, Clausen, and Miller 1965). Democratic supporters of McGovern in 1972, in addition to feeling very strongly about the Vietnam War, may have felt that McGovern's opposition to the increasingly unpopular war would carry him to the White House. Indeed, there is evidence that many McGovern activists at the 1972 Democratic national convention perceived him to be the strongest Democratic candidate (Stone and Abramowitz 1983).

An expected utility model of candidate choice provides a coherent theoretical explanation of how activists choose candidates in the nomination stage of the process. It recognizes that they may feel strongly about their ideological values and that the process is sequential with the real payoff coming not with the nomination victory, but with victory in the general election. As a result of the two-stage character of the process then, the expected utility model asserts that activists will consider the ideological utility each candidate would provide (the degree to which the activist agrees with the ideological positions of the candidates) and the chances each candidate has of winning the general election (Aldrich 1980; Coleman 1972; Aronson and Ordeshook 1972). As a result of considering these two factors, the utility-maximizing, or "rational," activist will support the candidate who appears to offer the best chance of providing the most ideological utility.

We defer a complete discussion of the model until Chapter 6, but it is important to recognize that the model differs rather substantially from the purist model. Under the purist model, the activist is predicted to support the candidate who best represents his ideological views. There is no room for compromise. Under the rational choice or utility-maximizer model, the activist weighs the ideological attractiveness of the candidates and their chances for victory in the general election. As a result of his desire to see his ideological preferences represented in government, the utility-maximizing activist may choose to support a candidate who is not his ideological favorite, but who offers the best chance of giving him some of what he wants. Thus compromising ideological preferences (rather than choosing to support a candidate who promises everything, but has less chance of winning) is a rational strategy in a sequential process. The model does not distinguish between "purists" and "professionals," nor is it motivated by an attempt to understand the changing context of nomination politics as a result of party reforms. All activists are assumed to be rational actors who understand the fundamental rules of the game and who seek to maximize their payoff from participating.

CONSEQUENCES OF THE MODELS
FOR PARTIES AND CANDIDATES

The purist and the rational choice models have very different consequences for the party organizations and for candidates for the parties' nominations. To suggest that the typical presidential activist is coming to fit the purist model is to suggest a change in nomination politics of massive import. Candidates seeking the nomination would have an incentive to emphasize relatively clearly stated ideological and issue positions. They would be forced to emphasize appeals to an audience not particularly concerned with the consequences of those appeals for the general election stage or for the political party. One consequence of purist politics would appear to be a proliferation of candidates, each attempting to build support within the party by appealing to specific issue, social, or ideological groups.

The party organizations may be jeopardized not only by the reforms that removed them from participating directly in nomination politics by promoting the primary system but also by the increased involvement of participants adopting the purist style. Because purists favor purist candidates, and because purist candidates eschew compromise, the accommodation necessary to successful coalition building in U.S. politics is made less likely. Purist candidates, such as Goldwater for the GOP in 1964 or McGovern for the Democrats in 1972, may, by their failure to appeal to a broad electoral coalition, effectively deed the White House to the opposition party. Losing elections, particularly by large margins and at the top of the ticket, does not help the parties. Intentionally nominating a weak candidate may positively hurt the party organizations by driving away from the party's coalition those interests that do not share the ideological preferences of the nomination winners. This reasoning has led a number of scholars who have accepted the purist model to be pessimistic about the health of the parties. Kirkpatrick (1976, pp. 152-53) saw the "new presidential elite" as threatening the endurance of the parties:

> The supporters of traditional candidates displayed
> the attitudes that the textbooks describe as char-
> acteristic of American political activists—intense
> concern for winning, achieving unity, party loyalty,
> and rewarding the faithful. These attitudes were
> significantly less common among the young, the
> inexperienced, and the supporters of the movement
> style of personalist/ideological candidates. The
> most straightforward interpretation of this con-
> figuration would seem to be that in 1972 we were
> moving away from a traditional organizational style
> toward one featuring parties that are less permanent,
> less broadly based, and less oriented toward winning.

Polsby and Wildavsky (1980, p. 285) expressed similar concerns about the consequences for the party organizations of a process dominated by purists:

> Without the desire to win elections, not at any cost
> but as a leading motive . . . there is no reason for
> politicians to pay attention to people. Winning,
> moreover, requires a widespread appeal that cannot
> be limited to just a narrow segment of the population.
> Thus the desire to win results in moderation in
> appeals to diverse groups in the electorate and in
> efforts to bring many varied interests together.
> This is why we prefer politicians to purists and
> parties of intermediation to parties of advocacy.

In brief, the parties lose in two ways in the postreform era. The reforms democratizing the process mean that the party organizations play a less active role in selecting nominees to represent them in the general election and may contribute to the increase in the number of purists active in nomination politics. Purists are themselves unwilling to compromise and are likely to be attracted to candidates who share their preference for straight talk and uncompromising ideological positions. To the extent that these kinds of candidates are favored by the contemporary process, the parties are likely to select unpopular nominees and suffer electoral defeat. Electoral defeat will not

help the party organizations against the myriad other forces
in the system that put them at a disadvantage.

Under the rational actor model, the consequences for the
candidates and parties are different from those that follow from
the purist model. Candidate strategies would appropriately
emphasize ideological positions, appealing to the personal preferences of activists, but candidates would also emphasize their
electability in the general election stage. This might cause
them to moderate their stands, asking activists to give up part
of their ideological ideal in order to allow the candidate to position himself in a way that will be favorable in the general election
(Brams 1978, pp. 134-45). Under the purist model, candidates
must appeal to activists without regard for the second stage.
Any hint that compromise might be necessary to appeal to the
general electorate would jeopardize support from purist activists.
Under the rational choice model, candidates run in the nomination stage in order to run in the general election. Thus they
can ask their activist supporters to compromise in order to
increase their chances in the general election.

Political parties trying to build a majority coalition should
have an easier time if the expected utility model is more valid
than the purist model. As long as there are numerous candidates
for the presidential nomination, the party will remain on the
sidelines for the first stage. Candidates will have strong
incentives to build their own personal organizations during that
stage, and the nomination winner will tend to rely upon his
organization in the general election phase. But the party's
interest in nominating a winner is not in nearly as great jeopardy
in the expected utility model as in the purist model. The party's
need to compromise, and its interest during the general election
in mobilizing activists who may have supported a nomination
loser during the first stage, should be easier to realize if the
expected utility formulation turns out to be accurate. The concerns of scholars like Kirkpatrick, Polsby, and Wildavsky about
the consequences of contemporary nomination politics for the
parties' involvement in presidential selection and governance
will not be completely removed, but a process dominated by
rational actors rather than purists should go a long way toward
ameliorating their concerns.

Briefly, then, the two models of presidential activists
offer differing views of how activists will choose to support a
candidate for their party's nomination. The purist model emphasizes the importance of ideological purity. This model, supported
by a number of survey studies of activists, asserts that activists
single-mindedly pursue their ideological interests in supporting

a candidate and that they do not anticipate the demands of the party or the electorate during the general election. They would rather be "right" and lose than compromise and win. The rational choice model, based upon the concept of "expected utility" asserts that activists will compromise their ideological principles in order to increase the chances of getting part of what they want. Because the process is sequential, they will take the general election stage into account when choosing candidates in the nomination stage. Activists, therefore, have two goals: promoting their ideological interests and winning. Their candidate choices will reflect both of these goals, not merely the first.

FOCUS OF THE BOOK

All of this concern about presidential activists may seem misplaced in an era dominated by presidential primaries (and, hence, primary voters) rather than caucuses, conventions, and smoke-filled rooms (and, hence, party activists). The percentage of votes cast in the 1968 Democratic and Republican nominating conventions by delegates selected by primary was 38 and 34 percent respectively. By 1980 the Democrats saw 71 percent of their national convention delegate votes cast by those selected in primary states whereas the Republican proportion had jumped to 76 percent (Ceaser 1982, p. 33). But even in an age dominated by the primary, there is good reason to be concerned about what motivates activists. Candidates depend upon (and, hence, will respond to) activists who provide them with support such as money and canvassing, typically unavailable from the run-of-the-mill primary voter. Some would say candidates need activist cadres in primary states even more than in nonprimary states because activist support is necessary to reach the primary voter. Moreover, understanding activists' motivations for supporting candidates for the nomination provides insights about possible alternatives to the direct primary. Many scholars and participants in presidential politics are convinced that the proliferation of presidential primaries is an undesirable development, and they seek to "reform the reforms."[1] Most postreform reform proposals call for greater participation by party activists, with reduced influence for primary voters. Of course, if activists are predominantly purist in style, changing the process to increase their influence may not solve the problems most worrisome to scholars like Polsby and Wildavsky, but such reform proposals at the very least should be informed by careful research on what motivates activists in their candidate choices.

Our concern is with coming to a more complete explanation of party activists' candidate choice during the nomination stage of the presidential selection process. Do activists behave as the purist model predicts? Or, do they have a real interest in winning the general election and, therefore, weigh electability as well as their ideological and issue preferences? Answering these questions is important because nominating presidential candidates is the most important function of the national political parties. The answers we offer will contribute to the ongoing debate about what to do about the contemporary nomination process. Understanding the way activists choose candidates will help us to understand the consequences of changing the process to increase the participation of party activists and to reverse the trend toward intraparty democracy in the form of primaries. Ours is the first study of presidential activists that employs survey research to study candidate choice and that explicitly recognizes the thinking of rational choice scholars about the process.

Our evidence results from surveys of delegates to 22 state presidential conventions in 11 states during the spring and summer of the 1980 campaign (the technical details of the study are described in the appendixes). These states utilized the caucus-convention method rather than the presidential preference primary to select delegates to the national conventions. We readily admit at the outset that the state parties included in our study are not necessarily representative of all 50 states. We have an excellent representation of states that use the caucus-convention method of selecting national convention delegates, but these states are themselves not completely representative of the nation. Urban midwestern and northeastern states are notable among the kinds of states we wish were better represented in our sample. The states included in our study vary in geographical location, population, economic development, and partisan orientation. Moreover, the design we used enabled us to reach a very large number of presidential activists (N = 17,628) relatively easily by contacting them at state nominating conventions.

While we cannot argue ours is a probability sample of all presidential activists (it is difficult to imagine how such a sample might be drawn), we believe our results are of general interest beyond the 11 states in the study. The contemporary presidential nomination campaign is national in scope even when candidates are focusing their resources upon a single state. Early in the campaign, the attention devoted to Iowa (a state included in our study) results not from the intrinsic importance of Iowa nor from the fact that it is somehow "typical" (it is not). Rather, Iowa is important because it is early, and thus can be the start of a candidate's drive toward national prominence and front-runner status. The same could be said of the New Hampshire primary. Candidates run in the national media by running in particular primary and caucus-convention states. V. O. Key, Jr. (1958, p. 413), in his text on the political parties written before the reforms of the process in the early 1970s, noted substantial differences between party organizations in presidential primary as compared with caucus-convention states. In his text written after the period of reform had taken hold, Frank Sorauf (1980, p. 273) emphasized the similarities between the two methods of national delegate selection:

> [T]he whole question of the alternative route to the nomination seems less and less important simply because the politics of the delegate search under primary and nonprimary conditions seem more and more alike. . . . In short, we have had a convergence of the two delegate selection processes into a more lengthy, more homogeneous, more important, and more expensive preconvention politics.

The national media, the open character of the process, and the general interest in the nomination campaign all have served to nationalize the process so that variations between primary and caucus-convention states are likely to be muted. Of course, there may be substantial variation across states with the degree of attention candidates devote to the state and with regional or ideological features of the state's parties. We present much of our analysis on the national level as well as on a state-by-state basis so the reader is free to judge the extent to which interstate variation may qualify our argument.[2] Of course, the extent to which our findings permit generalization to other states not included in our study is a matter of conjecture. Perhaps more important than the technical limitations of our sample is the fact that the data were collected during the 1980 presidential campaign, a campaign we believe uniquely suited to this sort of study of activists' candidate choice, but an election that was unique nonetheless.

THE 1980 ELECTION AS CONTEXT
FOR THIS RESEARCH

Probably the most important feature of the 1980 nomination campaigns from the perspective of understanding activists' candidate choice was that there were spirited contests for the nomination in both political parties. In both parties, there was a clear front-runner, but there were also plausible and well-organized challenges to the leading contender. There were reasonably sharp ideological and issue differences between the contenders in both parties, and each of the major candidates presented different styles and electoral strengths. These features of the campaign will allow us to compare our analysis across the two parties and to test some well-accepted propositions in the conventional wisdom of political science. Our evidence will challenge some of these propositions, modify and extend others, and confirm still others.

On the Democratic side, an incumbent president's right to represent his party for a second time against the Republicans was seriously challenged. Most observers agreed at the time that Jimmy Carter was vulnerable for several reasons. By very early in the nomination campaign, inflation had soared to record levels, impeaching Carter's credibility as manager of the economy. His image of vacillation and inconsistency in foreign affairs was for a time altered with the Iranian crisis precipitated by the seizure of the U.S. embassy in Tehran on November 4, 1979. Later in the nomination campaign, and especially in the general election against Reagan, the hostage crisis would haunt his candidacy. Perhaps the clearest indication of Carter's weakness was his consistently poor showing in polls against Senator Edward Kennedy during the summer and early fall of 1979 (Abramson, Aldrich, and Rohde 1982, p. 20). Indeed, Kennedy's apparent popularity within the Democratic Party for the 1980 presidential nomination was surely critical in convincing the Massachusetts senator to make a run for the presidency, after he had rejected the idea in several earlier nomination campaigns.

If Carter appeared vulnerable, he also had several advantages that together contributed to his eventual renomination. Most importantly, Carter was the incumbent. He utilized this advantage extensively, particularly early in the nomination campaign when he caught and passed Senator Kennedy in the polls. The Iranian hostage crisis permitted him the opportunity to issue a "nonpolitical" call for support and to follow a "Rose Garden" strategy early in the campaign. He was able to deny Kennedy the possible advantage of head-to-head campaigning in places like Iowa and New Hampshire where surrogates campaigned on his behalf. He withdrew from a scheduled "candidate forum" in Iowa just before the precinct caucuses, pleading that the hostage crisis demanded his full attention. Apparently as the result of appearing "presidential" (something incumbents can obviously do much more readily than challengers), Carter's standing in the polls and the party steadily grew. In the eyes of many political scientists familiar with the work of Anthony Downs (1957), Carter's other major advantage was that his ideological positions were relatively moderate. He was therefore well situated ideologically to appeal to the bulk of the U.S. electorate, particularly if the Republicans were to nominate the relatively extreme Ronald Reagan. The lessons of the 1964 nomination of Barry Goldwater and the Democratic nomination of George McGovern in 1972 were not lost on those familiar with Downs' book: nominate an extremist, and the opposition will capture the center and walk away with an easy November victory. Because Carter was in the center and an incumbent besides, he appeared to be in a strong position to claim the nomination.

Assessing Carter's strengths and weaknesses points up complementary assets and liabilities of Senator Kennedy. Carter's moderate policies, for example, while well suited as a base for his ideological appeal to the general electorate, left him vulnerable during the nomination campaign dominated by many relatively liberal Democratic activists and primary voters. Kennedy did not hesitate to emphasize the ideological differences between himself and the president, labeling Carter a closet Republican. As in Ronald Reagan's attempt to win the GOP nomination from Gerald Ford in 1976, Kennedy apparently hoped to appeal to the ideological preferences of activists and primary participants against a sitting president who had forsaken his partisan constituency.

Kennedy's traditional liberalism probably hurt him with some Democrats because 1980 was considered a year in which the liberal philosophy was unpopular. Moreover, once Kennedy declared his candidacy, problems with his image immediately surfaced. He could not duck the consequences of Chappaquiddick and related questions about his personal morality and leadership qualities. His image problems with the electorate at large may have been offset in part by the draw of the Kennedy name among Democrats and strong support from constituencies within the party such as organized labor and blacks. His attempt to portray Carter as an outsider in the Democratic Party worked for a time, but his own weaknesses as a candidate must have raised serious questions in the minds of activists as they decided whom to support for the Democratic nomination.

Jerry Brown, after a halting start in Iowa and New Hampshire, failed to get his campaign established, apparently falling prey to his image as a "flake." Early on it was clear that the Democratic Party would choose between the moderate incumbent Jimmy Carter and the liberal challenger Edward Kennedy. In their choice, activists were offered candidates rather different in ideological preferences and personal styles, as well as candidates with differing (but hardly overwhelming) electoral strengths.

The Republicans, too, faced an interesting problem in choosing from among a large field of contenders for the nomination. Ronald Reagan, after a strong challenge to Gerald Ford for the 1976 GOP nomination, was the front-runner with a large constituency within the party, but a number of other contenders including Congressman John Anderson, Senator Robert Dole, Senator Howard Baker, John Connally, Phillip Crane, and George Bush were unwilling to concede the nomination to the former California governor. Reagan's candidacy was strengthened by his ability to project himself well on television, by his appeal to Republican activists' conservative ideology, and by his impressive electoral record in California. In a nomination process dominated by purists, he could be expected to do very well despite the fact that other Republican leaders such as John Anderson and Gerald Ford suggested that his brand of conservatism would hurt him in the general election. Again, among those who link ideological moderation to electoral strength (and ideological "extremism" to electoral weakness) Reagan's brand of conservatism appeared to be an important liability. His other principal liabilities were his age, questions about the depth of his knowledge about public affairs, and his lack of experience holding national office.

Among the remaining candidates in the GOP field, competition for "contender" status was fierce. John Connally, for example, spent large sums of money early in the campaign, focusing primarily upon South Carolina as his proving ground. When he lost in the primary there despite this effort, his candidacy died. George Bush followed a strategy based on Carter's 1976 effort to emerge from the pack early and thereby capture attention. Bush accordingly emphasized Iowa and New Hampshire, devoting most of his personal attention and organizational resources to the first caucus and primary states respectively. His success in Iowa (he was the plurality winner just ahead of Reagan in the precinct caucus preference polls) sustained him through a loss in New Hampshire. John Anderson claimed to be the most liberal of the GOP candidates and, hence, the most electable in the second stage when conservative candidates would appear out of step with the electorate. The candidacies of Baker, Dole, and Crane quickly lost their steam as they were unable to establish their credibility with primary voters or activists. Bush's victories in Iowa and Massachusetts established his position as the principal alternative to Ronald Reagan, although John Anderson's strong showing was a constant irritant from the left.

Table 1.1 shows the first preferences of the activists in our study for their party's nomination at the time our surveys were conducted. It is immediately clear that for the 11-state "national" sample, Carter was the first choice of a substantial majority of Democratic activists while Reagan was the first choice of an even larger majority of Republicans. Together with their principal challengers, Kennedy on the Democratic side, and Bush on the GOP side, the top two candidates account for 88 and 89 percent of the first choice preferences in the two parties. As a result of the clear "major contender" status of Kennedy and Bush in their respective parties, we focus almost all our attention on the activists indicating a first choice preference for Carter or Kennedy, or Reagan or Bush. The table also presents the candidate preferences of activists in each of the state parties included in our survey.[3] For the most part, variation in activists' preferences across the 11 states is not of concern to us in this book. Some possible sources of that variation are immediately evident from Table 1.1, however. Southern states such as South Carolina and Virginia more strongly preferred Carter over Kennedy than Northern states such as North Dakota or Maine where Kennedy was relatively strong. Reagan's strength, not surprisingly, was greatest in the West and South. George Bush's strength was greatest in Iowa and Maine, two early states where he concentrated his organizational effort. Likewise, John Connally's concentration of effort in South Carolina apparently resulted in his greatest, though still small, proportion of activist support.

In some respects, the Republican campaign was the mirror image of the Democratic race. On the Democratic side, the front-runner was the relatively moderate Carter whereas on the Republican side the leading contender was the candidate generally perceived to represent the conservative (and, therefore, "extreme") wing of his party. The challenger for the Democratic nomination based his appeal in large measure on his ideological affinity with Democratic activists and primary voters. George Bush on the Republican side distinguished himself from Reagan by attempting to portray him as out of step with the

TABLE 1.1

Candidate Preference for Party's Nomination among Activists in the 11-State Survey

	National	Arizona	Colorado	Iowa	Maine	Missouri	North Dakota	Oklahoma	South Carolina	Texas	Utah	Virginia
Democrats												
Carter	61%	53%	44%	61%	40%	70%	48%	81%	86%	67%	57%	80%
Kennedy	27	43	32	30	32	20	40	14	10	26	30	16
Brown	2	1	2	1	13	1	1	1	1	1	2	0
Other Dem.	6	2	13	7	7	9	11	1	1	0	8	3
Anderson	1	1	2	1	0	0	4	0	1	0	3	0
Undecided	3	0	7	1	7	0	5	1	0	6	0	0
n =	(8,103)	(324)	(924)	(1,547)	(1,045)	(294)	(531)	(560)	(531)	(397)	(386)	(1,564)
Republicans												
Reagan	73	90	76	44	22	92	74	85	81	NA	91	74
Bush	16	6	12	32	58	2	18	5	8	NA	4	15
Anderson	2	0	2	6	6	1	4	0	0	NA	1	1
Baker	2	1	2	10	3	2	1	1	1	NA	1	1
Connally	2	0	1	2	4	0	0	4	6	NA	0	1
Crane	1	2	2	4	0	1	0	4	2	NA	0	1
Other Repub.	2	2	5	2	4	2	2	0	3	NA	2	4
Undecided	1	0	0	0	4	0	1	0	0	NA	0	0
n =	(7,961)	(376)	(612)	(1,042)	(440)	(368)	(399)	(1,185)	(703)	(564)	(1,176)	(1,660)

Note: n's reported are unweighted. Weighted file used to calculate percentages for the national sample.

American people and the purveyor of ill-considered "voodoo economics." Bush emphasized his own relative moderation and, thus, his appeal to a constituency beyond the Republican rank and file.

If we were to employ the purist model to predict candidate choice in the two parties, Kennedy and Reagan would appear to be the candidates most likely to have appealed to amateurs whereas Carter and Bush should have drawn support from the pragmatists in their parties. That Carter and Reagan were the favorites in our sample of activists (and won their nomination races) might be taken to mean that pragmatists were in control of the Democratic Party in 1980 whereas once again purists had gained ascendancy in the GOP. In this view, the principal difference between the purist Republicans of 1980 and their 1964 counterparts in the GOP or the 1972 Democrats was that the 1980 Republican purists, in nominating Ronald Reagan, also nominated a candidate who went on handily to win the general election.

In contrast to the purist model, the rational choice theory would explain support for the candidates as a function of expected utility calculations made by presidential activists. In this view, Carter and Reagan must have won their nomination campaigns because the expected utilities activists associated with them were greater than for their opponents. This would mean that the two eventual nominees promised enough ideological satisfaction and were judged electable enough to justify support. Such a conclusion would contradict the consensus in the literature reviewed above that purists have come to dominate the nomination process. Purists would be unlikely to consider the electability of a candidate in making their choice, and they would not compromise their ideological preferences in order to nominate a winner. In the case of the Democrats nominating Carter, the expected utility model has some face validity. He was a moderate incumbent, and Kennedy had obvious liabilities associated with his image. If the Democrats acted according to the rational choice formulation, however, one consequence would be to suggest that the purist wing of the party is in decline.

Among the Republicans, the rational choice model has little intuitive appeal. Their choice of Reagan appears to be a choice of an ideologically extreme contender, without regard for the consequences during the general election. Indeed, rational choice theorists consistently assert that candidates who adopt immoderate ideological views will be very unlikely to win the general election (Coleman 1972; Brams 1978). Given the visibility of the contemporary nomination process, it is likely candidates' ideological positions are relatively fixed in the minds of voters, regardless of any efforts they may make to change after the nomination (Page 1978).

Two explanations for the GOP choice of Ronald Reagan are possible: the Republican activists were purists who did not worry about Reagan's electability, or they rejected the assumption that moderate candidates like George Bush are more electable than ideologically extreme candidates like Ronald Reagan. If the first possibility is correct, we must accept the purist model for the Republicans (even though Reagan went on to win the White House), and reject the expected utility formulation. If the second possibility provides the best fit with the data, we can accept the rational choice explanation of preconvention candidate support, although we may wish to question the proposition that moderates are generally perceived to be stronger candidates than extremists.

PLAN OF THE BOOK

We proceed in the following chapters through an analysis of questions related first to the purist model of activists' candidate choice during the nomination period and then to the rational choice model. Throughout, we remain attentive to the implications of the questions we raise and the evidence we present for the health of the political parties and the nature of contemporary nomination politics. We believe that U.S. national politics is, on balance, more likely to be healthy with vital party organizations participating in nomination politics than without such parties. Therefore, we view with some alarm the thesis current among many close observers of U.S. politics that the parties are in decline. We have no reason to challenge much of the evidence that supports that thesis. The parties are doubtless weaker in the U.S. electorate than they were a generation ago. The increasing importance of presidential primaries has meant the parties necessarily play a less active role in selecting the nominees who will represent them against the opposition party in the general election. An increasingly sophisticated, media-centered, and high-technology style of campaign also means the parties are less important than they once were as mediators between candidates and voters. These developments contribute to the decline of the parties, and we present no evidence to question any of them.

Beyond the above features of the "party decomposition" thesis, however, the matter of how activists choose from among contenders for the nation's highest office has direct relevance for the health or decline of the party organizations. The purist model, if correct, suggests a process dominated by participants interested in pursuing their own ideological and issue concerns and not much interested in compromising to extend their coalition. In such a process, compromise is likely to be difficult, and a large number of contenders for the nomination, each appealing to relatively narrow interests, seems likely. In brief, then, we assume that a party dominated by activists choosing nominees in ways consistent with the purist model will be less likely to nominate electable candidates. We further assume that nominating electable candidates (and winning elections) contributes to the health of a party organization. Nominating candidates who cannot win contributes to the decline of the parties.

Chapters 2 and 3 examine questions directly related to the purist model as it is usually formulated in the literature. Chapter 2 examines the thesis that an important consequence of opening up the nomination process has been to generate incentives for candidates to appeal directly to social and interest groups for support. We test for a relationship between activists' social and interest group backgrounds and their candidate preference. In Chapter 3 we consider several dimensions of the amateur party activists: their experience in and commitment to the party organization, the incentives they had for becoming involved in the 1980 nomination campaigns, and their orientation toward ideological purity and compromise. Because the purist model emphasizes the latter dimension, we focus our analysis on the extent to which experience and incentives explain activists' orientation toward ideological purity and winning, and we examine the relationship between activists' purism and their candidate preference.

The remaining chapters present analysis based upon what we believe is a research strategy superior to that usually found in the survey literature on presidential activists. Rather than employ survey indicators that rely upon activists' own judgments about how much they value ideological purity versus compromise, or how important it is for political parties to do what is necessary in order to win elections, we use precise measures of activists' ideological preferences and their judgments about the electability of each presidential contender. These candidate-specific measures are used to explain the preferences activists express between the major contenders for their party's nomination. Chapter 4 explores the ideological bases of activists' candidate preferences. We summarize familiar evidence of the ideological and issue differences between the parties and then move on to an exploration of how 1980 party activists perceived the major candidates on the ideological scale and how their own ideological preferences influenced their candidate choices. Obviously, the story is complete if the purist model is correct and activists merely translate their ideological and issue preferences into a candidate preference. But such is not the case. In Chapter 5 we analyze the perceptions activists had of each contender's chances of winning the November election and present some possible explanations of why their perceptions of candidate electability varied. We then turn to an assessment of the effect of perceived candidate electability on candidate choice and how it compared with ideology in its effect. In Chapter 6 we present a rational choice model of candidate preference. We argue in light of the evidence presented in the earlier chapters, that an expected utility model is the most plausible way to think about activists' choice. We demonstrate that the model is vastly superior to the purist model in explaining candidate preference, and we suggest as a result of our research some of the consequences of this new evidence for the party organizations and for the character of nomination politics in the years ahead.

NOTES

1. An extensive literature concerns itself with possible alternatives to the current system dominated by primaries. See the first number of Commonsense (1982) for a report on the Conference on the Parties and the Nominating Process; Kirkpatrick (1978) and Ceaser (1982) as examples.

2. Most of the analysis reported below has been replicated on a state-by-state basis, although we do not report all of this analysis in order to avoid taxing the patience of the reader. The most interesting cases of variation across states have been reported, and where no such variation exists, or where there is no particular reason to expect it to exist, we refrain from presenting our nonfindings.

3. Because of an oversight in the questionnaire administered to Texas Republicans, we do not have a measure of their candidate preferences. Texas Republicans are included in our analyses of variables other than candidate preference.

2

SOCIAL AND GROUP INFLUENCES
ON CANDIDATE CHOICE

Democratic political parties are often described as coalitions of social interests. The type of coalition supporting a party is a major determinant of its ideological orientation and issue positions. In the United States since the New Deal, the Democratic Party has received disproportionate support from blue-collar workers, racial minority groups, urban dwellers, Catholics, Jews, and union members. White-collar workers, rural voters, business interests, and white Protestants have generally been the most reliable supporters of the Republican Party. Although the loyalty of these groups to the two major parties has varied from election to election, their relative support for Democratic and Republican candidates has remained fairly consistent (Axelrod 1972; 1974). The ideological and issue positions of the two parties have varied from election to election, and the differences between them have blurred at times, but the relative liberalism of the Democratic Party and the relative conservatism of the Republican Party have consistently reflected the differences between the social interests that comprise each party's electoral coalition.

Given the social bases of the parties, and the importance of the social makeup of the parties for their ideological orientations, it is appropriate to begin our investigation of the purist model with an analysis of the social bases of candidate preference. In the postreform era, with its proliferation of candidates competing for the nomination within the party, the purist model predicts that candidates will appeal to narrow interests within the parties, because activists will not be willing to compromise their ideological interests. As a result, nomination campaigns are likely to be characterized by conflict among ideological and social constituencies within the party.

Just as an uncompromising ideological style may undermine the party organization, intraparty conflict based upon social or interest group loyalties may fragment the party's electoral coalition. Since the 1960s, a number of new interest groups have entered the political arena alongside the more traditional economic interest groups such as business, labor, and agriculture. Women's rights advocates, antiabortionists, environmentalists, and even born-again Christians have become active in party affairs, attempting to use the party organizations to advance their own issue or ideological concerns. In contrast to the representatives of more traditional economic interest groups, these new interests often appear to be rather dogmatic in their approach to politics. Their apparent unwillingness to bend their principles for the sake of party unity is consistent with the purist model.

Reforms of the presidential nomination process may have increased the potential for intraparty divisiveness based upon social or interest group loyalties. Typically low turnout in primaries may enhance the influence of well organized groups (Lengle 1981). Similarly, the reformed caucus-convention process may encourage participation by special interest activists. The result, according to critics of the current nomination process, is to encourage the participation of purist activists in party nomination politics (Polsby and Wildavsky 1980). These purists are likely to be more concerned about the goals of specific social interests (such as religious, gender, or racial groups), or special group interests (environmentalists, prolife groups) than about their party and its success against the opposition.

REPRESENTATION OF DEMOGRAPHIC GROUPS

One of the simplest ways of assessing the character of the political parties as coalitions of social interests is by examining the social background characteristics of party activists themselves. This approach assumes that social background characteristics such as age, sex, or race stand for differences in political experiences and political values and that the behavior of party activists will be influenced by such experiences and values. Political scientists have long been concerned with the relationship between social background characteristics and the behavior of political elites (Matthews 1954; Edinger and Searing 1967; Putnam 1976, chap. 2), although the findings in this area have been mixed. In recent years, the two major parties, and especially the Democrats, have become quite concerned about the representation of certain demographic groups that were not well represented among the ranks of party leaders or activists in the past; the Democrats went as far as adopting what amounted to a quota system for the representation of young people, women, and racial minorities at their 1972 national convention. Although the Democrats watered down requirements for demographic representativeness after 1972, both parties have sought to increase participation by women, youth, and racial minorities since 1972 through "affirmative action" guidelines (Marshall 1981, pp. 36-42). For their 1980 national convention, the Democrats mandated that 50 percent of each state's delegation be made up of women.

The assumptions underlying these reform efforts are that members of different demographic groups have different political interests and values, and therefore, if party activists are more representative of the demographic characteristics of the population, they will also be more representative of the political interests and values of the population. As critics of party reform such as Kirkpatrick (1976; 1978) have noted, these assumptions are highly questionable. Nothing guarantees that the women, young people, or blacks who are chosen as delegates to party conventions will reflect the political views of their demographic counterparts in the population. Furthermore, the party activists may continue to be highly unrepresentative of the demographic characteristics of the electorate in other respects such as income, occupational status, and educational attainment.

Our 1980 state convention surveys included a series of social background questions. The characteristics included in the survey were age, sex, race, religion, education, and family income. (Occupation was not included because of the difficulty of obtaining precise occupational information in a self-administered questionnaire.) Based on the delegates' answers to these social background questions, we can compare the demographic characteristics of Democratic and Republican activists in our 11 states. The findings presented in Table 2.1 indicate that both sets of activists were highly educated and relatively affluent compared with the population as a whole. According to the 1980 census, an average of 16.6 percent of the residents over 25 years of age in the 11 states in our survey had completed four years of college (United States Department of Commerce 1982, p. 484). In contrast, slightly over half of the delegates in each party had finished college whereas one-fourth of the Republicans and one-third of the Democrats had continued their schooling beyond college. According to the census, an average of 26.3 percent of all households in these 11 states had incomes of $25,000 or

TABLE 2.1

Social Characteristics of Democratic and Republican Delegates

	Democrats	Republicans
Age		
18-29	20%	14%
30-39	28	22
40-59	37	46
60+	14	18
Sex		
Male	51	60
Female	49	40
Race		
White	88	98
Black	8	1
Other	4	1
Religion		
Protestant	65	84
Catholic	22	11
Jewish	2	1
Other, none	11	4
Education		
High school or less	18	15
Some college	28	32
Graduated college	20	26
Postcollege	33	27
Family Income		
Under $25,000	50	38
$25,000-$45,000	37	39
Over $45,000	13	23
(minimum n)	(10,071)	(9,922)

Note: Weighted n is shown. Actual n of cases is approximately 80 percent of weighted n.

more in 1979 (United States Department of Commerce 1982, p. 505). Among the delegates, one-half of the Democrats and three-fifths of the Republicans reported a household income of over $25,000. Although Republican activists were somewhat wealthier on average than Democratic activists, both parties recruited their delegates disproportionately from the educated upper-middle-class stratum of U.S. society.

Despite the similarity of the two groups of activists in terms of educational attainment and economic status, there were some noticeable differences between their demographic characteristics. In addition to being somewhat more affluent on average than the Democrats, Republican delegates were also somewhat older and included a smaller proportion of women in their ranks. This appears to reflect the greater emphasis placed by the Democratic Party in recent years on increasing the representation of these two groups in party affairs. Even more striking is the almost complete absence of members of racial minority groups from the ranks of Republican Party activists. Nonwhite party activists were concentrated almost exclusively in the Democratic Party. Finally, reflecting the traditional pattern of support for the parties in the electorate, larger proportions of Catholics, Jews, and other non-Protestants were found among Democratic activists than among Republican activists.

In general the demographic portrait of the two parties that emerges from Table 2.1 is of a quite homogeneous group of Republican activists and a somewhat more diverse group of Democratic activists. Republican delegates in these 11 states were predominantly male, affluent, middle-aged or older, white Protestants with a college education. Democratic delegates, although as well-educated as their Republican counterparts, were somewhat less affluent and included larger contingents of women, young people, racial minorities, and non-Protestants.

An examination of selected demographic characteristics of Democratic and Republican activists in each of the 11 states included in our survey generally reinforces the impressions gained from the overall results. Table 2.2 reveals considerable variation from state to state in the demographic characteristics of Democratic and Republican delegates. However, the relative degree of representation of demographic groups in the two parties was fairly consistent across these 11 states. In almost every state the Democratic delegates included larger contingents of young people and women. In every state, larger proportions of Republican delegates reported family incomes above $35,000. In every state, members of racial minorities and non-Protestants were better represented among Democratic activists than among Republican activists.

TABLE 2.2

Selected Social Characteristics of Democratic and Republican Delegates by State

State (minimum n)	Percentage of Delegates											
	Under Age 30		Female		Nonwhite		Protestant		College Graduates		Over $35,000 Income	
	Dem.	Rep.	Dem.	Rep.	Dem.	Rep.	Dem.	Rep.	Dem.	Rep.	Dem.	Rep.
Maine (953/397)	21	13	52	44	2	0	34	73	54	56	14	20
Iowa (1,560/1,003)	23	14	50	37	2	1	56	85	46	57	21	40
Missouri (286/328)	16	16	49	43	5	2	72	87	41	45	29	36
N. Dakota (560/350)	24	9	47	34	2	1	63	80	50	45	29	50
S. Carolina (529/677)	18	14	59	36	38	2	88	94	60	61	27	35
Texas (413/505)	21	13	40	45	16	3	67	82	60	59	32	55
Virginia (1,547/1,562)	18	15	51	47	18	2	78	82	59	57	36	48
Oklahoma (553/1,135)	18	20	53	48	12	4	84	89	37	40	28	34
Arizona (313/341)	22	4	47	47	20	2	46	79	58	46	23	31
Colorado (955/599)	18	8	50	40	9	3	52	78	58	59	25	43
Utah (411/1,134)	22	22	38	22	5	1	77	99	56	59	18	22

Note: Unweighted minimum n is shown. First n is for Democrats, second n is for Republicans.

The findings presented in Table 2.2 also reinforce our impressions of the relative social diversity of the two parties. In every state, Republican activists were overwhelmingly white and Protestant. In contrast, the proportions of racial minority members and non-Protestants among Democratic activists varied considerably across the 11 states. In several states with large black and/or Hispanic populations, such as South Carolina, Texas, Virginia, and Arizona, substantial proportions of black and/or Hispanic delegates were present at the Democratic conventions.

Having compared the social background characteristics of Democratic and Republican activists and examined variations in these characteristics across our 11 states, it remains to be seen whether these characteristics had any effect on the most important activity of these state convention delegates—the selection of a presidential candidate. If differences in social background characteristics stand for differences in political interests and if the candidates seeking a party's nomination appeal to different political interests within the party, then these background characteristics should have substantial effects on candidate choice among activists.

In the contest for the Democratic nomination in 1980, the two principal contenders, Jimmy Carter and Edward Kennedy, did base their campaigns on appeals to different political interests within the Democratic Party. Kennedy, in challenging the renomination of an incumbent president, based his campaign largely on an appeal for a restoration of the party's traditional liberal agenda that, he claimed, had been abandoned by President Carter. As an insurgent candidate making a liberal ideological appeal, we would expect Kennedy's campaign to have appealed most strongly to groups associated with antiestablishment party reforms and liberal issue concerns within the Democratic Party: the young, women, and members of racial minority groups. In sharp contrast with 1976, Jimmy Carter sought renomination in 1980 as the established leader of the Democratic Party. Given his relatively moderate ideological stance and his position as the incumbent, we would expect Carter's campaign to have appealed most strongly to more established and conservative groups within the Democratic Party: older, white, male party activists.

The findings presented in Table 2.3 provide only limited support for our hypotheses concerning the effects of social background characteristics on candidate choice among Democratic activists in 1980. Younger Democrats did provide greater support for Kennedy than older Democrats. However, even among

TABLE 2.3

Candidate Choice by Social Characteristics, Democratic
Delegates

	Percentage of Delegates Supporting			
	Carter	Kennedy	Other or Un- decided	(n)
All Democrats	61	27	12	(10,065)
Age				
18-29	48	38	14	(2,010)
30-39	58	28	14	(2,780)
40-59	66	23	11	(3,423)
60+	74	18	8	(1,363)
Sex				
Male	60	27	13	(5,067)
Female	63	27	10	(4,721)
Race				
White	61	26	13	(8,541)
Black	74	23	3	(676)
Other	43	54	3	(427)
Religion				
Protestant	71	20	9	(6,087)
Catholic	48	40	12	(2,064)
Jewish	42	37	21	(214)
Other, none	38	35	27	(1,062)
Education				
High school	65	27	8	(1,722)
Some college	60	29	11	(2,701)
Graduated college	57	29	14	(1,868)
Postcollege	61	25	14	(3,217)
Income				
Under $25,000	57	30	13	(4,691)
$25,000-$45,000	65	24	11	(3,425)
Over $45,000	67	21	12	(1,196)
Region				
North	52	30	18	(3,712)
West	51	35	14	(2,739)
South	79	17	4	(3,613)

Note: Weighted n shown. Actual n of cases is approximately
80 percent of weighted n.

the youngest group of activists, those under 30 years of age, Carter defeated Kennedy by a substantial margin. Differences in candidate choice between male and female activists were slight and in the opposite direction to our hypothesis: women gave slightly more support to the incumbent than men. Similarly, nonwhite Democratic activists were almost identical to white activists in their candidate preferences. Members of racial minority groups other than blacks (principally Hispanics) were the only demographic group who favored Kennedy over Carter. However, black activists in our survey gave Carter an even greater margin over Kennedy than white activists.[1]

Along with age, religious affiliation had a moderate impact on candidate choice among Democratic delegates. Jimmy Carter received his strongest backing from Protestant delegates while Edward Kennedy received disproportionate support from Catholics, Jews, and other non-Protestants (primarily individuals with no religious affiliation). Although religion was not an issue in the campaign for the Democratic nomination, the incumbent's evangelical Protestant beliefs had been widely publicized and may have accounted for his greater appeal among his coreligionists than among non-Protestant activists.

Finally, in addition to the social background characteristics included in the delegate survey, we also classified delegates according to their region. Of the 11 states included in the survey, four were classified as northern (Maine, Iowa, Missouri, and North Dakota), four as southern (Virginia, South Carolina, Texas, and Oklahoma), and three as western (Colorado, Arizona, and Utah). Table 2.3 shows that Jimmy Carter received stronger support from Democratic activists in his native region, the South, than in the rest of the country. Even in the North and West, however, Carter enjoyed a substantial margin over his challenger.

Two general conclusions can be drawn from the findings presented in Table 2.3. The first is that Edward Kennedy's campaign failed to attract very strong support even from Democratic activists who might have been expected on the basis of their social background characteristics to form the natural constituency of a liberal, insurgent candidate. The second conclusion is that social background characteristics were rather poor predictors of candidate choice among Democratic activists in 1980.

With the exception of John Anderson, who eventually left the Republican nomination campaign to run as an independent, all the GOP candidates in 1980 advocated varying degrees of conservatism. However, the two candidates who emerged as the leading contenders for the nomination, Ronald Reagan and George Bush, provided some contrast both in political style and ideology. Reagan, the clear front-runner for the nomination because of his strong challenge to Gerald Ford in 1976, had long been the champion of the party's right wing. Bush, seeking to inherit the support of those Republicans who had remained loyal to Gerald Ford in 1976, sought to project a more moderate and pragmatic image than Reagan, while remaining within the conservative mainstream of the party.

We have already seen that Republican activists in our 11 states were rather homogeneous in their social background characteristics. They were also rather uniform in their candidate preference: 73 percent of the delegates favored Ronald Reagan compared with only 16 percent for his closest competitor, George Bush, and 11 percent scattered among several other contenders or undecided (see Table 1.1). Moreover, Table 2.4 shows that there was relatively little variation in support for the two leading contenders among various demographic groups. Reagan was the overwhelming choice of almost every subgroup. Only among the tiny group of Republican activists who professed no religious affiliation did Reagan's support fall substantially below 60 percent.

Table 2.4 indicates that support for Reagan was somewhat greater among Republican activists who did not finish college than among those with college degrees. This may reflect the stronger appeal of Reagan's populist brand of conservatism among less well-educated Republican activists than among those with more years of schooling. However, even among Republicans who had continued their education beyond college, almost two-thirds backed Reagan's nomination. Likewise, George Bush did considerably better in the four northern states in our study (Maine, Iowa, Missouri, and North Dakota), than in the South (including Virginia, South Carolina, Texas, and Oklahoma) or the West (Colorado, Arizona, and Utah). This probably reflected Ronald Reagan's strong appeal to conservative Republicans in the South and the Rocky Mountain states as well as loyalty on the part of westerners to a native son. However, even in the northern states, where George Bush's relatively moderate brand of conservatism might have been expected to have greater appeal, Reagan defeated Bush by an overwhelming 58 to 28 percent margin.

As in the case of Democratic activists, social background characteristics do not seem to be strongly related to candidate choice among Republican state convention delegates. However, in order to assess the overall impact of demographic characteristics on candidate selection as well as the relative importance of each of our social background variables, we performed separate

TABLE 2.4

Candidate Choice by Social Characteristics, Republican
Delegates

| | Percentage of Delegates Supporting | | | |
	Reagan	Bush	Other or Undecided	(n)
All Republicans	73	16	11	(9,651)
Age				
18-29	68	18	14	(1,293)
30-39	67	19	14	(2,115)
40-59	75	15	10	(4,260)
60+	76	16	8	(1,734)
Sex				
Male	74	14	12	(5,726)
Female	70	19	11	(3,735)
Race				
White	72	16	12	(9,257)
Nonwhite	82	7	11	(150)
Religion				
Protestant	74	16	10	(7,744)
Catholic	73	16	11	(1,001)
Other, none	47	28	25	(461)
Education				
High school	80	13	7	(1,404)
Some college	78	13	9	(2,974)
Graduated college	69	20	11	(2,412)
Postcollege	65	20	15	(2,531)
Income				
Under $25,000	74	15	11	(3,453)
$25,000-$45,000	72	17	11	(3,420)
Over $45,000	69	20	11	(1,912)
Region				
North	58	28	14	(3,896)
West	86	8	6	(2,895)
South	80	9	11	(2,860)

Note: Weighted n shown. Actual n of cases is approximately
80 percent of weighted n.

33

discriminant analyses of candidate choice for Republican and
Democratic delegates, using the entire set of seven social background variables as predictors.[2] The discriminant analysis
attempts to classify delegates according to their candidate
choice on the basis of their demographic characteristics. Because the overwhelming majority of Democratic and Republican
delegates supported one of the two leading contenders for their
party's nomination, with the remaining delegates scattered among
several minor candidates or undecided, we included in the analyses only those Democrats who supported Carter or Kennedy and
only those Republicans who supported Reagan or Bush. Table
2.5 presents the results of the discriminant analyses for Democratic and Republican delegates. The standardized discriminant
function coefficients are analogous to the standardized regression
coefficients (beta weights) in ordinary regression analysis and
can be interpreted as estimates of the relative importance of
each demographic variable in the classification of delegates
according to candidate support. Among the Democratic activists,
age, religion, and region had the greatest impact on candidate
choice. The results are consistent with the zero-order relationships examined earlier: older delegates, Protestants, and
southerners were more likely to support Carter; younger delegates, non-Protestants, and nonsoutherners were more likely
to support Kennedy. After controlling for the other demographic
variables, nonwhites were slightly less likely to support Carter
than whites. However, the overall predictive power of the
analysis is relatively poor. The canonical correlation coefficient,
which is analogous to the coefficient of multiple correlation (R)
in multiple regression analysis, is only .34 with all seven demographic variables in the analysis. This confirms our impression
that social background characteristics had relatively little influence on candidate choice among Democratic activists in 1980.

The results of the discriminant analysis for Republican
delegates are also consistent with the findings examined earlier.
Region was by far the strongest predictor of candidate choice:
activists from the northern states were less likely to favor Ronald
Reagan over George Bush than those from the southern or western states. In addition, higher levels of educational attainment
were related to support for Bush. Once again, however, the
overall impact of the seven social background variables on candidate choice was quite limited, as indicated by the canonical
correlation of .35.

TABLE 2.5

Discriminant Analysis of Candidate Choice with Social Background Variables

Social Background Variable (direction)	Democrats (n = 6,276)	Republicans (n = 6,157)
Age (older)	.468	.151
Sex (male)	-.007	.294
Race (nonwhite)	-.272	.040
Religion (Protestant)	.511	.066
Education (higher)	.073	-.423
Income (higher)	.197	-.067
Region (non-South for Democrats, North for Republicans)	-.549	-.913
% Correctly classified	64.5	70.6
Canonical correlation	.34	.35

Note: Actual n of cases shown. Analysis based on weighted n. Candidate choice variable scored in direction of Carter for Democrats, Reagan for Republicans. Entries in table are standardized discriminant function coefficients.

INTEREST GROUP REPRESENTATION

In addition to their social background characteristics, party activists may be influenced by their involvement in organized interest groups. Such groups have a vital stake in the selection of candidates sympathetic to the issue or ideological concerns of their members. In the United States, organized interest groups play active roles in the nominating processes of the major parties as well as in general election campaigns. We are interested in examining the representation of organized interest groups among Democratic and Republican party activists in 1980: to what extent were various interests represented at the state party conventions, and what effect did this have on the selection of candidates by the parties? Although representation of organized interest groups is necessary in order to build electoral coalitions, parties may be harmed if they become captives of interest groups that place their own issue or ideological concerns before the viability of the party.

In order to examine interest group representation among Democratic and Republican state convention delegates, the survey instrument included a list of 11 types of organizations. The delegates were asked to indicate which of these organizations they had been politically active in. This was an attempt to measure active and politically relevant group involvement. It appears from the results presented in Table 2.6 that these party activists were also actively involved in a large variety of political interest groups and organizations. Including a residual category of "other issue-related groups," the average Democratic delegate reported active involvement in approximately 2.2 groups while the average Republican delegate reported active involvement in approximately 1.7 groups. Even allowing for some exaggeration and rather broad interpretations of what constituted politically active involvement, there appears to have been a substantial level of interest group representation at these Democratic and Republican conventions.

There were substantial differences between the two parties in the representation of certain interest groups. These differences were generally consistent with the parties' traditional electoral coalitions and ideological positions. Labor unions, teachers' organizations, and liberal issue groups (civil rights, women's rights, and environmental groups) were much better represented among Democratic activists than among Republican activists. Business interest groups, religious groups, and antiabortion groups were found in larger numbers at Republican conventions than at Democratic conventions.

The delegates in both parties represented a broad range of political interests. No single group came close to achieving a majority in either party. As in the case of delegates' social background characteristics, however, we find greater diversity among the Democrats than among the Republicans. Very few members of labor unions or liberal issue groups were found among the ranks of GOP activists. In contrast, Democratic activists did include fairly sizeable contingents representing business interest groups and religious organizations.

A comparison of interest group representation at Democratic and Republican conventions across our 11 states again reveals considerable variation from state to state within each party. However, the relative degree of representation of these groups in the two parties was fairly consistent. Table 2.7 shows that labor unions, teachers' organizations, and liberal issue groups were better represented at the Democratic conventions in all 11 states, while business organizations were better represented at the Republican conventions in all 11 states. Antiabortion activists

TABLE 2.6

Interest Group Representation among Democratic and Republican Delegates

	Democrats	Republicans
Labor unions	17	3
Education organizations	27	14
Other professional groups	22	22
Business organizations	15	26
Religious organizations	28	36
Women's rights groups	18	4
Civil rights groups	19	2
Environmental groups	15	8
Public interest groups	24	17
Antiabortion groups	6	10
Farm organizations	12	13
(n)	(11,011)	(10,985)

Note: Weighted n shown. Actual n of cases is approximately 80 percent of weighted n. Entries are percentages of Democratic and Republican delegates reporting active involvement in each type of group.

were found in greater numbers among Republican delegates than among Democratic delegates in every state except Maine and North Dakota. Labor union activists and representatives of liberal issue groups were scarce at all 11 Republican conventions. In every one of these states, a greater variety of interest groups was represented among Democratic activists than among Republican activists. Republican presidential activists in 1980 were relatively homogeneous in their organizational affiliations as well as in their social characteristics when compared with Democratic activists.

The evidence examined thus far indicates a considerable amount of interest group activity among both Democratic and Republican state convention delegates in 1980. To what extent did this activity influence the most important responsibility of the delegates, the nomination of a presidential candidate? The growing involvement of liberal and conservative issue groups in party affairs in recent years has aroused concern on the

TABLE 2.7

Interest Group Representation among Democratic and Republican Delegates by State

	Unions		Education		Business		Women's Rights		Civil Rights		Ecology		Anti-abortion	
	Dem.	Rep.	Dem.	Rep.	Dem.	Rep.	Dem.	Rep.	Dem.	Rep.	Dem.	Rep.	Dem.	Rep.
Maine (1,046/441)	17	3	22	20	12	19	15	3	15	2	17	11	8	4
Iowa (1,673/1,107)	21	2	25	18	8	27	21	9	14	4	14	12	7	8
Missouri (317/380)	23	6	24	10	18	25	12	3	10	3	14	7	8	13
N. Dakota (623/404)	7	1	28	16	10	35	13	5	8	1	14	5	10	8
S. Carolina (621/739)	7	2	33	11	22	25	19	2	32	2	10	9	3	8
Texas (440/564)	23	2	30	10	18	29	20	3	26	3	19	7	4	10
Virginia (1,669/1,716)	13	2	26	11	16	24	18	4	25	2	11	7	2	11
Oklahoma (609/1,244)	15	3	35	12	18	22	22	5	20	2	12	6	6	10
Arizona (337/387)	22	2	29	11	14	29	20	3	25	1	15	6	5	14
Colorado (1,003/638)	16	4	20	13	13	27	19	4	19	3	18	8	4	9
Utah (452/1,218)	26	5	23	20	11	25	15	4	14	1	17	4	6	20

Note: Unweighted n is shown. First n is for Democratic delegates, second n is for Republican delegates. Entries are percentages of Democratic and Republican delegates in each state reporting active involvement in each type of group.

part of scholars and party leaders that the new activists may be more concerned with promoting the issue or ideological concerns of their group than with the viability of the party and its electoral success.

We would expect the two principal contenders for the Democratic presidential nomination in 1980 to have appealed to activists in different types of interest groups. Edward Kennedy, whose challenge to the incumbent was based largely on his liberal record and positions, should have done relatively well among delegates active in liberal issue-groups such as women's rights, civil rights, and environmental organizations, while Jimmy Carter, as an incumbent with a relatively moderate record and positions, should have done best among delegates associated with more traditional economic interest groups such as business, labor, and agricultural organizations.

The findings presented in Table 2.8 only partially support our expectations regarding interest group activity and candidate

TABLE 2.8

Candidate Choice by Interest Group Involvement, Democratic Delegates

Type of Group	Percentage of Democrats Supporting			
	Carter	Kennedy	Other, Undecided	(n)
All Democrats	61	27	12	(10,065)
Unions	49	39	12	(1,794)
Education	67	22	11	(2,739)
Professional	60	29	11	(2,234)
Business	71	19	10	(1,473)
Religious	66	24	10	(2,840)
Women's rights	54	34	12	(1,812)
Civil rights	50	38	12	(1,931)
Environmental	46	33	21	(1,522)
Public interest	59	28	13	(2,392)
Antiabortion	58	28	14	(564)
Agricultural	60	25	15	(1,219)

Note: Weighted n is shown. Actual n of cases is approximately 80 percent of weighted n.

support among Democratic activists in 1980. Members of the
newer, liberal issue-groups were more likely to support Edward
Kennedy and less likely to support Jimmy Carter than other
Democrats. However, the differences were not very large, and
Carter defeated Kennedy by a clear margin in every group.
Once again it appears that Kennedy's campaign failed to develop
strong support even among those Democratic activists who,
based on their interest group affiliations, should have formed
his natural ideological constituency. Turning to the more traditional economic interest groups, we find that delegates active
in business organizations did support Jimmy Carter more strongly
than other Democrats. However, Democrats active in agricultural organizations were very similar to other delegates in their
candidate preferences, and labor union activists were less likely
to support Carter and more likely to support Kennedy than
other Democrats. Although the labor movement has been associated with opposition to party reforms supported by liberal
activists in recent years, many union activists, alienated by
the Carter administration's economic policies, supported Edward
Kennedy's challenge to Jimmy Carter's renomination in 1980.
Moreover, unlike earlier liberal insurgent candidates such as
Eugene McCarthy and George McGovern, Kennedy had strong
ties to organized labor. Nevertheless, despite dissatisfaction
with the incumbent's economic policies and close connections
between the challenger and union leaders, Jimmy Carter defeated
Edward Kennedy among union activists by a decisive 49 to 39
percent margin. The overall impression gained from Table 2.8
is that interest group involvement had relatively little impact
on candidate choice among Democratic activists in 1980.

In the contest for the Republican nomination, we would
expect Ronald Reagan to have received his strongest support
from party activists associated with conservative interest groups.
George Bush, as the principal moderate alternative to Reagan,
should have received his strongest backing from the relatively
small number of GOP delegates active in liberal issue-groups.
The findings presented in Table 2.9, however, provide only
limited support for these hypotheses. Ronald Reagan decisively
defeated George Bush among every group of Republican activists,
although his margin was somewhat reduced among the small group
of GOP delegates associated with women's rights or environmental
interest groups. Reagan's margin over Bush was only slightly
larger among delegates active in religious organizations than
among other Republicans, despite the strong support given to
the former California governor by some conservative evangelical
ministers. Only among antiabortion activists was Reagan's margin

TABLE 2.9

Candidate Choice by Interest Group Involvement, Republican Delegates

| Type of Group | Percentage of Republicans Supporting | | | |
	Reagan	Bush	Other, Undecided	(n)
All Republicans	73	16	11	(9,651)
Unions	74	13	13	(281)
Education	65	22	13	(1,377)
Professional	69	19	12	(2,122)
Business	75	15	10	(2,544)
Religious	77	14	9	(3,514)
Women's rights	50	26	24	(413)
Civil rights	69	15	16	(203)
Environmental	61	25	14	(729)
Public interest	72	16	12	(1,660)
Antiabortion	90	3	7	(1,028)
Agricultural	79	13	8	(1,288)

Note: Weighted n shown. Actual n of cases is approximately 80 percent of weighted n.

over Bush substantially greater than his overall margin. Reagan's strong endorsement of a constitutional amendment to prohibit abortion gained him the backing of 90 percent of the right-to-life activists. This group constituted the closest approximation to a monolithic single-issue voting bloc in either party. With this exception, though, interest group involvement appeared to have relatively little impact on candidate choice among Republican activists in 1980.

In order to assess the overall impact of interest group involvement on candidate choice as well as the relative importance of involvement in different types of groups, discriminant analyses were performed for Democratic and Republican delegates, using 12 different group activity questions (the 11 groups included in Tables 2.8 and 2.9 along with a residual category labeled "other issue-related group") to predict candidate preference. The results presented in Table 2.10 are generally consistent with the impressions gained from our examination of the zero-

TABLE 2.10

Discriminant Analysis of Candidate Choice with Organizational Activity Variables

Type of Organization	Democrats (n = 6,276)	Republicans (n = 6,157)
Labor union	-.456	.076
Education	.387	-.347
Professional	-.115	-.219
Business	.382	.151
Religious	.238	.205
Women's rights	-.206	-.408
Civil rights	-.506	.038
Environmental	-.247	-.411
Public interest	.072	-.032
Antiabortion	.002	.638
Agricultural	-.056	.253
Other issue-group	-.085	.116
% correctly classified	64.8	68.6
Canonical correlation	.25	.23

Note: Actual n of cases shown. Analysis based on weighted n. Candidate choice variable scored in direction of Carter for Democrats, Reagan for Republicans. Entries in table are standardized discriminant function coefficients.

order relationships in Tables 2.8 and 2.9. Among Democratic delegates, involvement in unions and liberal issue-groups was associated with greater support for Edward Kennedy while involvement in business and education interest groups was associated with greater support for Jimmy Carter (the latter relationship undoubtedly reflecting the strong backing given to the incumbent by the largest teachers' organization, the National Education Association). However, the overall impact of interest group activity on candidate preference among Democratic delegates was very weak as demonstrated by the canonical correlation of .25 with all 12 activity variables in the analysis. Involvement in interest groups had even less of a bearing on candidate choice among Democratic delegates than social background characteristics.

The results of the discriminant analysis for Republican delegates are very similar to those for Democrats. Involvement in antiabortion groups did increase the likelihood of supporting Ronald Reagan. To a lesser extent, involvement in environmental or women's rights organizations increased the likelihood of supporting George Bush. Overall, though, our 12 interest group activity measures were poor predictors of candidate choice. The canonical correlation of .23 indicates that among Republican activists, just as with many Democratic activists, interest group involvement had even less impact on candidate preference than social background characteristics.

SUMMARY AND CONCLUSIONS

There were important differences between the social background characteristics of Democratic and Republican presidential activists in 1980. Although both parties' state convention delegates tended to be highly educated and affluent compared with the general population, Republican delegates were generally older and wealthier than their Democratic counterparts. The GOP delegates were also predominantly male and overwhelmingly white and Protestant while Democratic delegates included larger contingents of women, non-Protestants (Catholics, Jews, and individuals with no religious affiliation), and nonwhites (principally blacks and Hispanics). In general, Republican activists were quite homogeneous in their social background characteristics while Democratic activists were somewhat more diverse.

An examination of the organizational affiliations of these presidential activists also revealed substantial differences between the two parties. Although a wide variety of interest groups was represented in both parties, labor unions, education organizations, and liberal issue-groups (civil rights, environmental, and women's rights organizations) were much better represented among the ranks of Democratic activists than among GOP delegates; business, religious, and antiabortion groups were generally better represented at Republican conventions than at Democratic gatherings. Once again, Democratic activists showed greater diversity in their organizational affiliations than Republican activists: very few members of labor unions or liberal issue-groups were found at any of the Republican conventions in our 11 states; in contrast, business and religious organizations were generally well-represented at Democratic conventions.

Despite the high level of interest group activity among Democratic and Republican delegates, we found little justification for the fears of some scholars that, as a result of recent reforms, party activists may place the issue or ideological concerns of organized interest groups before the electoral success of the party. When it came to choosing a presidential candidate, interest group affiliation had very little impact on the behavior of either Democratic or Republican state convention delegates in 1980. Nor do our findings provide much support for the assumption underlying recent reforms aimed at making participants in the presidential nominating process more representative of the demographic characteristics of the electorate: social background characteristics such as race, sex, and age also had little bearing on the choice of a presidential nominee by Democratic or Republican activists.

Extending the purist model to include social and interest group bases of candidate choice does not provide much insight into what motivated presidential activists to support a nomination candidate in 1980. In the next chapter, we take up a more direct application of the purist model by examining activists' experience, motivations, and goals in relation to the party organization. The party itself, rather than demographic characteristics or interest group affiliation, may have been the most important reference group for party activists in defining their role in the presidential nominating process.

NOTES

1. Almost all the black Democratic delegates were from the four southern states in our survey—Virginia, South Carolina, Texas, and Oklahoma. This may explain the greater support for Carter among black activists than among whites.

2. In the case of a dichotomous dependent variable, such as our measures of candidate preference for Democratic and Republican delegates, ordinary least squares (OLS) regression analysis may produce biased estimates because of violation of the normal distributional assumptions underlying OLS estimation procedures. In the case of a dichotomous dependent variable, either probit analysis or discriminant analysis can be utilized, because the dependent variable can be treated as either ordinal or categorical. The estimates produced by these two techniques are very similar. For a comparison of regression, probit, and discriminant analysis, see Aldrich and Cnudde (1975).

3

PURISM AMONG
PRESIDENTIAL ACTIVISTS

The purist model described in Chapter 1 provides the
focus of this chapter. Our primary concern here is with the
model's expectations about how contemporary activists will
choose from among contenders for their party's nomination.
In that regard, the model asserts that purist activists will
support the candidate who best represents their ideological
and issue preferences and will refuse to compromise their values
in order to promote the welfare of the party or to nominate a
winning candidate. Purists thus adopt a "political style" that
represents their general orientation toward compromise in order
to win elections. Past studies of presidential activists have
found a link between political style and candidate choice, especially in the Republican nomination of Barry Goldwater in 1964
(Soule and Clarke 1970), the 1972 Democratic nomination of
George McGovern (Sullivan et al. 1974; Soule and McGrath 1975;
Kirkpatrick 1976), and the Reagan challenge to Gerald Ford in
1976 (Roback 1980).

Unfortunately, the literature contributing to the purist
model has defined the central concepts "amateurism" and "professionalism" in a variety of ways, with confusing results.
Soule and Clarke (1970) attempted to measure several different
dimensions of political style including support for intraparty
democracy, preoccupation with winning, willingness to compromise, and support for programatic parties. In addition, they
employed a self-characterization measure asking activists to
classify themselves as "someone who: (a) works for the party
year after year, win or lose and whether or not you like the
candidate or issues; or (b) works for the party only when there
is a particularly worthwhile candidate or issue" (Soule and
Clarke 1970, p. 890). Although a factor analysis of their items
produced four distinct dimensions, Soule and Clarke and others

(for example, Hoftstetter 1971; Soule and McGrath 1975; Roback 1975; Hitlin and Jackson 1977) have analyzed amateurism versus professionalism as a single, unidimensional orientation.

DeFelice (1981) has argued that amateurism versus professionalism does not involve a single orientation and that there is an important distinction between preoccupation with winning and commitment to the party organization. We have said in Chapter 1 that a party dominated by purist activists may suffer consequences that weaken the organization, but that argument demands a demonstration, first, that activists' candidate choice is in fact consistent with the purist model and, second, that research on the problem not confound orientation toward winning or losing with attitudinal or behavioral attachment to the party organization.

Because of our interest in candidate choice, we are concerned primarily with activists' attitudes toward the tradeoff between ideological purity and electoral success ("purism versus pragmatism"). This distinction between concern with advancing one's issue positions and interest in winning has been the central theme of literature based on the purist model since Wilson (1962) introduced his concept of "amateurism versus professionalism." It is the amateur activist's preoccupation with maintaining ideological purity at the expense of broad electoral appeal that, according to critics, constitutes a major threat to the viability of the parties as organizations.

In order to assess purist versus pragmatic orientations, our survey instrument included five items explicitly posing the tradeoff between ideological purity and broad electoral appeal. These items were very similar to ones used in previous studies to measure activists' relative concern with advancing their issue positions versus winning (Soule and Clarke 1970; Hofstetter 1971; Soule and McGrath 1975; Roback 1975; Hitlin and Jackson 1977; Kirkpatrick 1976). The results, presented in Table 3.1, were similar to those obtained in previous studies and indicate a predominance of purist orientations. On all five items, clear majorities of Democratic and Republican delegates chose ideological purity over broad electoral appeal. There were no consistent differences between the responses of Democratic and Republican activists to these items. In 1980, both groups of activists displayed overwhelmingly purist inclinations.

We combined our five items into an index measuring ideological purism.[1] This index can be used to compare the orientations of Democratic and Republican activists in each of the 11 states included in our survey. The findings presented in Table 3.2 indicate that, although there was some variation in purist

TABLE 3.1

Ideological Purism among Presidential Party Activists

Item	Democrats	Republicans
A political party should be more concerned with issues than with winning elections (Agree)	74%	68%
The party platform should avoid issues which are very controversial or unpopular (Disagree)	78	78
I'd rather lose an election than compromise my basic philosophy (Agree)	71	74
A candidate should express his convictions even if it means losing the election (Agree)	83	84
Broad electoral appeal is more important than a consistent ideology (Disagree)	55	65

Note: Entries shown are percentages of delegates in each party taking purist position on each question. Based on weighted n. Minimum weighted n = 9,987 for Democrats and 10,196 for Republicans.

versus pragmatist orientations among the 22 state parties, purist opinions predominated among all of these groups of presidential party activists. Even among the most pragmatic delegates, the Virginia Democrats and North Dakota Republicans, about three-fifths of the activists scored at the upper end of ideological purism (taking no pragmatic positions or only one pragmatic position on the five items). Nor were there any clear patterns to the variations observed among state parties. In some states, Democratic activists were more pragmatic than Republican activists, but in other states the Republicans were more pragmatic. There were no clear regional differences and delegates from strong state parties were neither more nor less pragmatic than delegates from weak state parties.

Thus far, our findings appear to confirm the fears of critics of presidential nominating reforms concerning the threat to the

TABLE 3.2

Ideological Purism by State Party

State (n)	Democrats	Republicans
Maine (925/375)	79%	72%
Iowa (1,448/994)	79	69
North Dakota (534/359)	75	59
Missouri (265/331)	70	76
Virginia (1,391/1,521)	62	70
South Carolina (528/664)	75	75
Texas (397/502)	70	70
Oklahoma (519/1,098)	75	80
Colorado (928/580)	74	74
Arizona (304/335)	68	67
Utah (417/1,125)	73	85

Note: Entries shown are percentages of delegates in each state party scoring high on index of ideological purism (0 or 1 pragmatic opinion on five items). Actual n shown for Democratic/Republican delegates.

parties posed by the influx of amateur activists more concerned with advancing their ideological convictions than with winning elections. Several factors may help to explain the predominance of purist orientations among contemporary presidential activists. The first is the incentives that motivate individuals to become active in the presidential nominating process. Kirkpatrick (1976) has argued that members of "the new presidential elite" are less interested in receiving some personal benefit from their involvement in the presidential campaign or in helping their party to achieve success than in promoting their issue positions or specific candidates who support these issue positions. As a result, these activists may be unwilling to compromise their ideological convictions or support a candidate who does not share their convictions, just to help their party win in November.

In order to assess motivations for participating in the presidential nominating process, we asked delegates attending state party conventions to rate the importance of a series of incentives for their involvement in the 1980 campaign.[2] As expected, "purposive" incentives—issue and candidate concerns—

were rated as the most important reasons for participating by Democratic and Republican delegates: 76 percent of Democratic activists and 84 percent of Republican activists rated issue concerns as a "very important" motivation; 71 percent of Democratic activists and 80 percent of Republican activists rated support for a particular candidate as "very important." In contrast, any personal benefits received from involvement in the campaign were rated as much less important by these delegates. Only 8 percent of Democratic delegates and 4 percent of Republican delegates indicated that advancing their own political careers was a "very important" motivation, and only 14 percent of Democratic delegates and 8 percent of Republican delegates rated the prestige and visibility of attending the state party convention as a "very important" motivation.

Despite the importance of issue and candidate concerns as motivations, delegates also rated party loyalty as an important factor in their decision to participate in the campaign: 62 percent of Democratic activists and 67 percent of Republican activists indicated that party loyalty was a very important reason for becoming involved in the nominating process. These results do not support Kirkpatrick's (1976) contention that issue and candidate concerns have replaced partisanship as motivations for activism among the "new presidential elite." Most state party convention delegates in 1980 displayed strong issue and candidate concerns and strong party loyalties.[3]

The strength of purposive motivations among Democratic and Republican delegates in 1980 might be expected to contribute to purist orientations among these activists. However, strong partisan motivations could counterbalance issue and candidate concerns by causing activists to weigh the consequences of their decisions for their party's electoral prospects. The correlations presented in Table 3.3 support these hypotheses: while strength of purposive motivation was positively correlated with ideological purism, partisanship was negatively correlated with purist orientations. However, although these correlations are in the expected direction and statistically significant, the relationships between delegates' motivations and their stylistic preferences are weak. The incentives that motivated individuals to become delegates are not very helpful in explaining their orientations toward the relative priority of winning versus maintaining ideological purity.

Another factor that may help to explain stylistic orientations among party activists is political experience. We would expect activists who have held party or elected office to display a greater concern with winning and a greater willingness to compromise

TABLE 3.3

Correlates of Ideological Purism

Variable	Democrats	Republicans
Political Experience		
Party experience	-.13	-.14
Office-holding	-.08	-.08
Incentives for Party Activity		
Purposive	.11	.14
Partisan	-.17	-.14
Personal	-.07	-.08
Ideology		
Extreme self-placement	.08	.12

Note: Entries shown are correlations (Pearson's r) between measures of experience, incentives, and ideology and index of ideological purism. Minimum weighted n = 8,321 for Democrats and 8,440 for Republicans.

their ideological convictions than activists without such experience. Recent reforms have diminished the role of elected and party officials in the presidential nominating process and allowed political newcomers to play a greater role in the selection of presidential candidates. These reforms may contribute to the predominance of purist orientations among contemporary presidential activists.

We asked state party convention delegates a series of questions about their current and past political activities. These questions were combined to form two indexes—one measuring party experience and one measuring public office-holding experience. About one-third of the delegates in each party had held some party office, mainly at the local level. Another third had been members of a local party committee, the most basic unit of party organization in the United States. One-third of the delegates had no party experience. About one-eighth of the delegates in each party had held some elective public office, mainly at the local level.

The correlations presented in Table 3.3 lend some support to our hypothesis concerning the relationship between political experience and stylistic orientation: there was a negative corre-

lation between both party and office-holding experience and
ideological purism among both Democratic and Republican delegates. However, once again, these relationships are weak.
Political experience does not clearly distinguish between activists
with purist orientations and those with more pragmatic orientations. Even among delegates who had held party or elected
office, purist orientations predominated: almost two-thirds of
the Democratic and Republican delegates with experience as
either party or elected officials scored high in ideological purism
(expressing no pragmatic opinions or only one pragmatic opinion
on the five items).

One additional factor that might help to explain stylistic
orientations among presidential activists is political ideology.
We might expect purist orientations to be most prevalent among
delegates with relatively extreme ideologies: extremists will
probably feel more intensely about their ideological views than
moderates and be less willing to compromise their convictions
in order to broaden their party's electoral appeal. This would
pose a threat to the parties as organizations because the issue
positions of extremist activists are probably very different from
those of most voters.

We measured ideological extremism by asking delegates to
place themselves on a five-point liberal-conservative scale.
Nineteen percent of Democratic delegates placed themselves at
the extreme left ("very liberal") position on this scale while
41 percent of Republican delegates placed themselves at the
extreme right ("very conservative") position on the scale.[4]
The correlations shown in Table 3.3 support our hypothesis
about the direction of the relationship between extremism and
purism. However, the correlations again are weak in both
parties: .12 among Republican delegates and .08 among Democratic delegates. Even among self-styled moderates in both
parties, purist orientations predominated. Sixty-nine percent
of "middle-of-the-road" Democratic activists and 62 percent
of "middle-of-the-road" Republican activists scored at the high
end of the ideological purism scale compared with 79 percent of
"very liberal" Democratic activists and 79 percent of "very
conservative" Republican activists.

Taken together, the findings presented in Table 3.3 indicate that purist attitudes were pervasive among presidential
activists in both parties in 1980. Given a choice in the abstract
between maintaining their ideological convictions or compromising
their beliefs for the sake of greater electoral appeal, the large
majority of presidential activists, regardless of experience,
motivation, or political philosophy, chose the course of ideological purity.

PURISM, PRAGMATISM, AND CANDIDATE CHOICE

The assumption underlying research on the stylistic orientations of party activists is that these orientations have practical
consequences for activists' behavior within the party organization: activists with "purist" orientations would be expected to
choose candidates based on their ideological convictions, regardless of the electoral consequences for the party. In 1980,
Ronald Reagan and Edward Kennedy ran strongly issue-oriented
campaigns for the Republican and Democratic presidential nominations. We would expect Reagan's campaign to have appealed
strongly to conservative purists among Republican activists
while Kennedy's campaign should have appealed strongly to
liberal purists in the Democratic Party.

Ronald Reagan was the overwhelming choice of the Republican activists in our 11-state survey. However, the findings
presented in Table 3.4 provide little support for the hypothesis
that Reagan appealed particularly to activists with purist orientations. After controlling for ideology, there was almost no
relationship between stylistic orientation and candidate choice
among Republican activists. Reagan was the overwhelming
choice of pragmatic as well as purist conservatives. Despite
his claim of broader electoral appeal as a moderate conservative,
George Bush received little support except among the small
group of moderate-to-liberal GOP activists. Even here, Bush
ran only even with Ronald Reagan.

The contest for the Democratic nomination was closer than
that for the Republican nomination in 1980. However, the findings presented in Table 3.4 indicate that Edward Kennedy's
brand of issue-oriented liberalism had only a limited appeal in
1980, even among liberal Democratic activists. There was only
a weak relationship between political style and candidate choice
among liberal Democratic activists: pragmatists were somewhat
more likely to support Jimmy Carter than purists. However,
Edward Kennedy's appeal was generally confined to the minority
of liberals who placed themselves on the extreme left of the
ideological spectrum; Kennedy was beaten decisively by Jimmy
Carter among purist as well as pragmatic moderate liberals.

In contrast to the findings reported by Soule and Clarke
(1970) regarding delegates to the 1968 Democratic national
convention and by Soule and McGrath (1975) regarding delegates
to the 1972 Democratic national convention, political style was
not strongly related to candidate preference among Democratic
or Republican state convention delegates in 1980. In 1980,
purist orientations predominated among all groups of candidate

TABLE 3.4

Candidate Preference by Stylistic Orientation and Ideological Self-Placement

	Democratic Delegates			
	Carter	Kennedy	Other, Undecided	(n)
Very Liberal				
Purist	23%	55%	22%	(897)
Mixed	40	48	12	(447)
Pragmatic	42	49	9	(344)
Fairly Liberal				
Purist	53	35	12	(1,482)
Mixed	59	28	13	(1,043)
Pragmatic	65	23	11	(950)
Moderate to Conservative				
Purist	75	14	11	(1,369)
Mixed	78	14	8	(1,076)
Pragmatic	78	13	9	(1,047)

	Republican Delegates			
	Bush	Reagan	Other, Undecided	(n)
Moderate to Liberal				
Purist	35	39	26	(407)
Mixed	38	39	23	(324)
Pragmatic	44	32	24	(379)
Fairly Conservative				
Purist	19	69	12	(1,581)
Mixed	19	71	10	(1,222)
Pragmatic	24	64	12	(1,250)
Very Conservative				
Purist	4	90	6	(1,724)
Mixed	4	90	6	(905)
Pragmatic	7	86	7	(703)

Note: Weighted n shown.

supporters in both parties: 70 percent of Democratic delegates supporting Jimmy Carter scored high on the ideological purism scale, compared with 78 percent of those supporting Edward Kennedy; 63 percent of Republican delegates supporting George Bush scored high on the ideological purism scale, compared with 75 percent of those supporting Ronald Reagan.

DISCUSSION AND CONCLUSIONS

Given a choice in the abstract between maintaining their ideological convictions or compromising their beliefs in order to help their party win an election, the overwhelming majority of Democratic and Republican presidential activists in 1980 chose ideological purity. Contrary to our expectations based on the work of James Q. Wilson and recent studies of national convention delegates, however, purist attitudes were not confined to politically inexperienced delegates, extremists, or activists motivated primarily by issue or candidate concerns. In 1980, purist attitudes were prevalent among all groups of presidential activists, regardless of experience, ideological orientation, or motivation. Furthermore, purist attitudes predominated among all groups of candidate supporters in both parties.

We might conclude from these results that the amateur activists first described by Wilson had completely captured control of both parties by 1980. Before accepting this conclusion, however, we must consider the question of what practical consequences follow from activists' adherence to ideological purism as a set of abstract principles. Our findings suggest that many activists do not connect these abstract norms with the practical task of choosing among candidates with varying ideological commitments and electoral prospects. In supporting the general principle of ideological purity, activists may be paying lip service to a set of values that are widely accepted in U.S. society: the belief that politics should be governed by principles rather than by self-interest. But this does not necessarily mean that activists are unconcerned about winning or losing. Instead of measuring activists' support for purist or pragmatic principles in the abstract, we need to assess the tradeoff between ideology and the pursuit of victory in connection with the choice of a presidential candidate.

NOTES

1. The correlations (Pearson's r) among these items ranged from .07 to .49, with an average of .23. The purism-pragmatism

scale was constructed by counting the number of "pragmatic" responses to the five items. Respondents with scores of 0 or 1 were classified as high on ideological purism, those with a score of 2 were classified as moderate, and those with scores of 3, 4, or 5 were classified as low on purism.

2. When these items were factor analyzed, two distinct factors emerged. The first factor included four items: career advancement, the excitement of the campaign, the opportunity to meet people, and the prestige of serving as a delegate. All of these items involve personal benefits received from participating in the campaign. The second factor included only two items: advancing issue concerns and working for a particular candidate. These two items clearly correspond to the more impersonal, or purposive motivations for participation. Two items—party loyalty and civic duty—did not load clearly on either factor. For a more in-depth analysis of delegates' incentives for participating in the 1980 nominating campaigns, see Abramowitz, McGlennon, and Rapoport (1983).

3. There was a positive correlation between purposive and partisan motivations in both parties ($r = .13$ for Republican delegates, $r = .23$ for Democratic delegates).

4. Only 3 percent of Democratic delegates described themselves as "very conservative," and less than 1 percent of Republican delegates described themselves as "very liberal."

4

THE IMPACT OF IDEOLOGY

The evidence presented in Chapter 3 indicated that Democratic and Republican activists in our 11 states tended to subscribe to "purist" values: given a choice in the abstract between ideological principles and electoral success, the large majority chose ideological principles. Furthermore, issue concerns were rated as the most important motivation for participating in the nominating process. These findings are consistent with many earlier studies of presidential activists that have found them to be overwhelmingly purist, particularly in the postreform era. Surely if the purist model is to explain activists' candidate preferences, we can expect ideology and issue preferences to be very strong predictors of candidate choice and electability to be weak. This chapter and the next examine the effects of ideology and electability.

The contests for the Democratic and Republican presidential nominations in 1980 presented party activists with choices between candidates with contrasting ideological orientations. On the Democratic side, a moderate incumbent was challenged for renomination by the most visible spokesman of the party's liberal wing. Edward Kennedy's challenge to Jimmy Carter was based largely on an appeal to liberal activists alienated by the incumbent's relatively conservative record and positions on issues such as national health insurance, military spending, energy price deregulation, and management of the economy. On the Republican side, the champion of the conservative cause within the GOP was opposed by a candidate offering a more moderate brand of conservatism. Ronald Reagan's position as the spokesman for the conservative wing of the party had been established during the 1964 presidential campaign when his oratory on behalf of Barry Goldwater gained him national recognition. George Bush emerged early in the primary-caucus season

as the principal alternative to Ronald Reagan by appealing for
the support of more moderate Republicans who had remained
loyal to Gerald Ford in 1976.

In order to examine the influence of ideology on the behavior of state convention delegates, we asked delegates to
place themselves on a five-point liberal-conservative scale
ranging from very liberal (1) to very conservative (5). We
also asked them to indicate their positions on 13 specific issues
including economic issues such as wage-price controls and oil/gas
price deregulation, social issues such as abortion and the Equal
Rights Amendment, and international issues such as the SALT II
Treaty with the Soviet Union and U.S. military involvement in
the Middle East.[1] Within each party, liberal-conservative self-
identification was related to delegates' positions on all 13 issues.
In addition, the results of factor analyses of all 13 issues along
with liberal-conservative self-placement indicated that it was
reasonable to locate Democratic and Republican delegates along
a single liberal-conservative continuum.[2]

The findings presented in Table 4.1 show that Democratic
and Republican delegates diverged sharply in their positions
on the five-point liberal-conservative scale. Almost 60 percent
of the Democratic delegates described themselves as very or
fairly liberal, while almost 90 percent of the Republican delegates
described themselves as very or fairly conservative. However,

TABLE 4.1

Ideological Self-Classification of Democratic and Republican
Delegates

Ideology	Democrats (n = 10,604)	Republicans (n = 10,729)
Very liberal	19%	1%
Somewhat liberal	39	3
Middle-of-the-road	22	9
Somewhat conservative	17	46
Very conservative	3	41
Total	100%	100%

Note: Weighted n shown. Actual n of cases is approximately
80 percent of weighted n.

as with social background characteristics and organizational affiliations, Republican delegates were more homogeneous than Democratic delegates in ideological self-identification; just over two-fifths of Democratic activists classified themselves as either moderate or conservative while only one-eighth of Republican activists classified themselves as either moderate or liberal. More than two-fifths of Republican delegates placed themselves at the most conservative point on the scale while less than one-fifth of Democratic delegates placed themselves at the most liberal point on the scale.

An examination of the positions taken by Democratic and Republican delegates on the 13 policy issues included in the survey reinforces the impressions gained from Table 4.1. Table 4.2 shows that Democratic activists were substantially more liberal than Republican activists on all 13 issues. The greatest interparty differences were on the Equal Rights Amendment, defense spending, national health insurance, affirmative action, and the SALT II Treaty. These were issues on which national party leaders, and especially presidential candidates, had taken opposing positions. Interparty differences were much smaller on the issues of abortion, draft registration, and increasing America's military presence in the Middle East, issues on which national party leaders and presidential candidates had not taken clearly opposing positions.

The findings presented in Table 4.2 also reinforce our impression of the relative ideological homogeneity of the two parties. On 12 of these 13 issues, Republican activists showed a higher level of agreement than Democratic activists; only on the issue of abortion were Republican activists more divided than Democratic activists. An average intraparty consensus score was computed for Democrats and Republicans by taking the average absolute difference between the percentage of delegates taking the liberal position on each issue and the percentage of delegates taking the conservative position on each issue. This score has a theoretical range of zero (complete disagreement) to one hundred (complete agreement). The average intraparty consensus score was much higher for Republican delegates than for Democratic delegates. Thus, Democratic activists were much more divided in their issue positions than Republican activists, just as they were much more divided in their ideological self-placement. Only on the issue of abortion was there a close division of opinion among Republican delegates. Only on the issue of the Equal Rights Amendment did Democratic delegates achieve a level of internal agreement approaching the average level of internal agreement among Republican delegates.

TABLE 4.2

Issue Liberalism of Democratic and Republican Delegates

Issue (liberal position)	Democrats (minimum n = 9,600)	Republicans (minimum n = 9,782)
Equal Rights Amendment (favor)	73	24
Antiabortion amendment (oppose)	65	48
Defense spending rise (oppose)	50	8
National health insurance (favor)	65	8
Nuclear power (oppose)	54	17
Domestic spending cuts (oppose)	56	19
Affirmative action (favor)	68	27
Oil/gas deregulation (oppose)	52	19
Wage-price controls (favor)	54	24
Higher unemployment to control inflation (oppose)	54	26
Draft registration (oppose)	37	21
Ratification of SALT II (favor)	63	15
Military presence in Middle East (oppose)	44	23
Average issue liberalism	57	21
Average intraparty consensus	19	57

Note: Weighted minimum n shown. Actual minimum n is approximately 80 percent of weighted n. Entries in table are percentages taking liberal position on each issue plus one-half of undecided percentage. National health insurance issue was not included in survey in Maine.

Table 4.3 presents the average ideological self-placement, issue liberalism, and intraparty consensus scores for Democratic and Republican delegates in each of the 11 states. There was considerable variation in ideology across states within each party. Democratic activists in Iowa and Arizona were substantially more liberal than Democratic activists in Missouri and Oklahoma; Republican activists in Maine and Iowa were substantially less conservative than Republican activists in Texas and South Carolina. However, despite these variations, the main impression left by Table 4.3 is of consistent interparty differences in ideology. In all 11 states, Democratic activists were much more liberal than Republican activists. The Maine Republicans, the most liberal group of Republican activists, were substantially more conservative than the Oklahoma Democrats, the most conservative group of Democratic activists. Regional differences in ideology within each party were relatively small: Democratic activists in the South were only slightly more conservative than Democratic activists in the North and West; Republican activists in the North were only slightly more liberal than Republican activists in the South and West.

In general, the activists within each party had similar ideologies regardless of what state they were from. In addition, Republican activists consistently showed greater intraparty agreement on issues than Democratic activists. In all 11 states, the intraparty consensus score for Republican delegates was higher than the score for Democratic delegates. The most ideologically divided Republican activists (in Maine and Iowa) were more cohesive in their issue positions than the most cohesive Democratic activists (in Iowa).

We are interested in the impact of ideology on candidate preference among Democratic and Republican presidential activists. A necessary condition for ideology to influence candidate choice is that delegates perceive some difference between the ideological orientations of the candidates seeking their party's nomination. In addition to asking delegates to place themselves on a five-point liberal-conservative ideology scale, we asked them to place the major candidates seeking the Democratic and Republican nominations on this scale. Figure 4.1 shows the average perceptions of the candidates' ideological positions by Democratic and Republican delegates. In both parties, the delegates did perceive a fairly clear ideological choice between the two leading candidates seeking the nomination. Democratic delegates viewed Edward Kennedy as substantially more liberal than Jimmy Carter; Republican delegates viewed Ronald Reagan as substantially more conservative than George Bush.[3]

TABLE 4.3

Ideological Positions of Democratic and Republican Delegates by State

State (minimum n)	Ideological Self-Identification		Issue Liberalism		Intraparty Consensus	
	Dem.	Rep.	Dem.	Rep.	Dem.	Rep.
Maine (966/415)	2.4	3.8	61	33	23	39
Iowa (1,584/1,060)	2.3	3.8	65	32	32	39
North Dakota (561/377)	2.4	4.1	61	24	24	52
Missouri (289/363)	2.7	4.1	50	20	16	60
Virginia (1,472/1,588)	2.5	4.3	55	22	23	58
South Carolina (543/697)	2.5	4.4	52	17	25	66
Texas (416/540)	2.4	4.5	57	15	22	70
Oklahoma (563/1,155)	2.8	4.4	46	18	22	64
Colorado (957/613)	2.3	4.3	59	21	21	60
Arizona (307/359)	2.2	4.4	63	18	30	65
Utah (424/1,151)	2.5	4.4	52	18	12	64

Note: Actual n shown for Democrats/Republicans. Ideological self-identification based on five-point liberal-conservative scale: 1 = very liberal, 5 = very conservative. National health insurance issue not included in Maine survey.

FIGURE 4.1

Perceptions of Candidates' Ideological Positions by Democratic and Republican Delegates

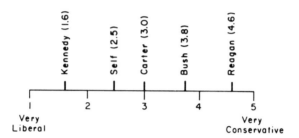

DEMOCRATIC DELEGATES

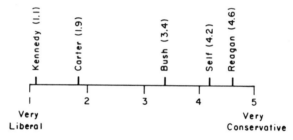

REPUBLICAN DELEGATES

Table 4.4 shows the relationship between ideological self-placement, positions on 13 national issues, and candidate preference, among Democratic delegates. Based on the delegates' perceptions of Edward Kennedy's and Jimmy Carter's ideological orientations, we would expect liberalism to be associated with support for Kennedy. The findings generally support this hypothesis, but the differences in candidate preference between delegates on opposing sides of these issues are often rather small. On every issue except draft registration, a majority or plurality of those taking the liberal side nevertheless supported Jimmy Carter. Even on the issue of national health insurance, with which Edward Kennedy had been closely associated, and on which his position contrasted sharply with the incumbent's, Kennedy trailed Carter among delegates taking the liberal (pro-national health insurance) position by a substantial margin.

TABLE 4.4

Candidate Preference by Ideology and Issue Positions,
Democratic Delegates

| Issue | Percentage of Democrats Supporting | | | |
	Carter	Kennedy	Other, Un- decided	(n)
Ideology				
Very liberal	34	50	16	(1,845)
Somewhat liberal	58	29	12	(3,809)
Moderate	75	16	9	(2,118)
Conservative	80	10	10	(1,850)
Equal Rights Amendment				
Favor	56	31	13	(6,795)
Oppose	76	14	10	(2,132)
Antiabortion Amendment				
Favor	67	23	10	(2,823)
Oppose	58	29	13	(5,826)
Defense Spending Rise				
Favor	76	16	8	(4,031)
Oppose	45	39	16	(4,216)
National Health Insurance				
Favor	50	39	11	(4,985)
Oppose	84	7	9	(2,252)
Nuclear Power				
Favor	75	16	9	(3,303)
Oppose	47	38	15	(4,229)
Domestic Spending Cuts				
Favor	74	16	10	(3,339)
Oppose	50	35	15	(4,527)
Affirmative Action				
Favor	55	33	12	(5,628)
Oppose	71	16	13	(2,146)
Oil/Gas Deregulation				
Favor	74	16	10	(3,429)
Oppose	48	39	13	(3,831)
Unemployment to Control Inflation				
Favor	74	16	10	(3,307)
Oppose	48	39	13	(4,098)

(continued)

Table 4.4 (continued)

Issue	Carter	Kennedy	Other, Un-decided	(n)
		Percentage of Democrats Supporting		
Wage/Price Controls				
Favor	49	40	11	(4,245)
Oppose	74	14	12	(3,490)
Draft Registration				
Favor	76	15	9	(5,481)
Oppose	35	46	19	(3,085)
SALT II Ratification				
Favor	58	29	13	(4,631)
Oppose	64	23	13	(2,110)
Military in Middle East				
Favor	73	19	8	(4,259)
Oppose	44	39	17	(3,085)
Issue Liberalism Scale				
1 (Most liberal)	18	65	17	(1,019)
2	46	40	14	(1,232)
3	61	29	10	(1,692)
4	75	17	8	(1,786)
5	86	7	7	(1,340)
6 (Most conservative)	85	4	11	(679)

Note: Weighted n shown. Actual n of cases is approximately 80 percent of weighted n. National health insurance issue was not included in survey in Maine.

Only among delegates who placed themselves at the "very liberal" position on the ideological self-placement scale did Edward Kennedy receive greater support than Jimmy Carter. Among the much larger group of moderate liberals, Carter enjoyed an overwhelming 58 to 29 percent lead. Similarly, when we combined our 13 issues into an overall issue liberalism scale, it was only among the small minority of Democratic delegates located at the most liberal end of the scale, those who were consistently liberal on almost every issue, that Edward Kennedy actually led Jimmy Carter. Here, as on the individual issues, we are left with the question of why Edward Kennedy failed to develop greater support among liberal Democratic activists.

In the contest for the Republican presidential nomination, we would expect Ronald Reagan to have appealed most strongly to Republican activists who shared his conservative views and philosophy while George Bush should have received the support of more moderate Republicans. The findings presented in Table 4.5 generally support this hypothesis, but, as in the case of Democratic activists, the relationships are rather weak. On every one of our 13 national issues, Ronald Reagan was the overwhelming choice of those delegates taking the conservative position. However, Reagan also led Bush among delegates who took the liberal position on each of these issues. Even among the small minority of Republican activists who described themselves as liberal or moderate in ideology, Bush managed only an even split with Reagan. Similarly, when we combined all 13 national issues into an issue liberalism scale, Ronald Reagan ran neck-and-neck with George Bush among the most liberal group of Republican delegates. It is not surprising that Ronald Reagan was the overwhelming choice of conservative Republican activists in 1980; it is surprising that he also made strong inroads among moderate-to-liberal activists.

How can we explain the relatively poor showings of Edward Kennedy and George Bush among those party activists who should have comprised their ideological constituencies? Perhaps these activists misperceived the candidates' ideological positions. By combining the questions asking delegates to place themselves on the five-point liberal-conservative scale with the questions asking them to place the major candidates on the same scale, we can construct a measure of relative ideological proximity to the two leading candidates in their party for Democratic and Republican delegates. Table 4.6 shows that there was a strong relationship between ideological self-placement and candidate proximity in both parties. The overwhelming majority of Democratic activists who placed themselves at the most liberal point on the scale viewed Edward Kennedy as closer to their own ideology than Jimmy Carter. Even among moderate liberals, Kennedy was favored over Carter by a decisive 51 to 24 percent margin. Only among moderate-to-conservative Democratic activists was Jimmy Carter preferred on ideological grounds to Edward Kennedy. Among all liberal Democratic activists, 72 percent viewed Edward Kennedy as closer than Jimmy Carter while only 18 percent viewed Jimmy Carter as closer than Edward Kennedy. These liberal Democratic activists clearly perceived Edward Kennedy as more liberal than Jimmy Carter and closer to their own ideological positions. Yet only 36 percent of them supported Kennedy for the nomination while 50 percent supported Carter.

TABLE 4.5

Candidate Preference by Ideology and Issue Positions,
Republican Delegates

| Issue | Percentage of Republicans Supporting | | | |
	Reagan	Bush	Other, Undecided	(n)
Ideology				
Liberal to moderate	38	39	23	(1,244)
Somewhat conservative	69	20	11	(4,434)
Very conservative	89	4	6	(3,729)
Equal Rights Amendment				
Favor	44	36	20	(1,995)
Oppose	82	10	8	(6,727)
Antiabortion Amendment				
Favor	86	8	6	(4,450)
Oppose	57	26	17	(3,979)
Defense Spending Rise				
Favor	76	15	9	(8,387)
Oppose	40	29	30	(464)
National Health Insurance				
Favor	77	11	12	(409)
Oppose	79	11	10	(7,452)
Nuclear Power				
Favor	76	15	9	(6,988)
Oppose	55	23	22	(938)
Domestic Spending Cuts				
Favor	76	14	10	(7,232)
Oppose	65	21	14	(1,463)
Affirmative Action				
Favor	62	22	16	(1,600)
Oppose	77	13	10	(5,822)
Oil/Gas Deregulation				
Favor	75	14	11	(6,709)
Oppose	65	22	13	(1,117)
Unemployment to Control Inflation				
Favor	72	16	12	(5,907)
Oppose	74	16	10	(1,592)
Wage-Price Controls				
Favor	71	20	9	(1,698)
Oppose	74	15	11	(6,500)

Table 4.5 (continued)

| Issue | Percentage of Republicans Supporting | | | |
	Reagan	Bush	Other, Undecided	(n)
Draft Registration				
Favor	73	16	11	(6,840)
Oppose	73	15	12	(1,544)
SALT II Ratification				
Favor	50	28	22	(788)
Oppose	78	13	9	(7,236)
Military in Middle East				
Favor	76	14	10	(6,184)
Oppose	61	23	16	(1,239)
Issue Liberalism Scale				
1 (Most liberal)	38	39	24	(1,184)
2	66	22	12	(2,859)
3	83	9	8	(3,221)
4 (Most conservative)	89	4	7	(1,141)

Note: Weighted n shown. Actual n of cases is approximately 80 percent of weighted n. National health insurance issue was not included in survey in Maine. Issue liberalism scale based on all issues except national health insurance.

There was also a strong relationship between ideological self-placement and candidate proximity among Republican activists. Moderate-to-liberal GOP delegates overwhelmingly viewed themselves as closer in ideology to George Bush than to Ronald Reagan. Even among moderate conservatives, more delegates placed themselves closer to Bush (37 percent) than to Reagan (28 percent). Only among very conservative Republican activists was Ronald Reagan overwhelmingly preferred to George Bush on ideological grounds. Among all other Republican activists, including liberals, moderates, and moderate conservatives, George Bush was preferred on ideological grounds to Ronald Reagan by a margin of 44 to 23 percent. Yet 62 percent of these activists supported Reagan's nomination while only 24 percent supported Bush.

The findings presented in Table 4.6 suggest that Democratic and Republican activists did not base their candidate preferences

TABLE 4.6

Perceived Ideological Proximity by Ideological Self-Classification

Closer to	Democrats			
	Very Liberal	Fairly Liberal	Moderate	Very, Fairly Conservative
Carter	5%	24%	78%	89%
No difference	8	25	16	7
Kennedy	86	51	6	5
Total	99%	100%	100%	101%
(n)	(1,640)	(3,367)	(1,748)	(1,560)

Closer to	Republicans		
	Moderate to Liberal	Fairly Conservative	Very Conservative
Reagan	6%	28%	86%
No difference	23	34	12
Bush	71	37	1
Total	100%	99%	99%
(n)	(1,122)	(4,205)	(3,732)

Note: Weighted n shown. Actual n of cases is approximately 80 percent of weighted n.

entirely on ideology. This conclusion is supported by Table 4.7, which shows the relationship between ideological proximity and candidate choice among Democratic and Republican delegates. Both Edward Kennedy and George Bush failed to win the support of large numbers of activists who were closer in ideology to them than to their opponents. In fact, a slight majority of Republican delegates who were closer in ideology to Bush supported Reagan for the nomination.

SUMMARY AND CONCLUSIONS

Both parties' presidential nominations in 1980 were decided by contests between candidates offering contrasting ideological

TABLE 4.7

Candidate Preference by Perceived Ideological Proximity

| Candidate Preference | Democrats | | |
| | Closer to | | |
	Carter	No Difference	Kennedy
Carter	90%	79%	39%
Kennedy	10	21	61
Total	100%	100%	100%
(n)	(3,228)	(1,083)	(2,643)

| Candidate Preference | Republicans | | |
| | Closer to | | |
	Reagan		
Reagan	95%	77%	51%
Bush	5	23	49
Total	100%	100%	100%
(n)	(3,587)	(1,712)	(1,719)

Note: Weighted n shown. Based on delegates supporting two leading candidates in each party.

positions. Yet, despite the strong issue orientations of Democratic and Republican activists, ideology cannot completely explain the decisive victories of Jimmy Carter and Ronald Reagan over their principal intraparty opponents, Edward Kennedy and George Bush.

Our survey of state party convention delegates in 11 states revealed a sharp ideological split between Democratic and Republican activists in 1980: Democratic delegates were predominantly liberal in their ideological orientations and issue positions; Republican delegates were overwhelmingly conservative in their ideological orientations and issue positions. In all 11 states, Democratic activists were substantially more liberal than Republican activists. The most conservative Democratic state convention delegates (in Oklahoma) were much more liberal than the most liberal Republican state convention delegates (in Maine and Iowa).

Republican activists also showed much greater consensus in their ideological orientations and issue positions than Democratic activists. Forty-two percent of Democratic delegates placed themselves at the center or right on the liberal-conservative scale while only 13 percent of Republican delegates placed themselves at the center or left on this scale. Likewise, GOP delegates showed greater consensus than Democratic delegates on 12 of 13 national issues (the one exception being the abortion issue). In all 11 states, Republican activists were more united in their issue positions than their Democratic counterparts.

Democratic and Republican delegates did perceive a fairly clear ideological choice between the two principal contenders for their party's nomination: Democrats viewed Edward Kennedy as substantially more liberal than Jimmy Carter, and Republicans viewed Ronald Reagan as substantially more conservative than George Bush. However, there were only weak to moderate relationships between activists' ideological orientations and issue positions and their candidate preferences. In general, liberal Democrats were more likely to support Edward Kennedy than moderate-to-conservative Democrats, and moderate-to-liberal Republicans were more likely to support George Bush than conservative Republicans. However, Jimmy Carter received considerable support from liberal Democratic activists, and Ronald Reagan made strong inroads among moderate-to-liberal Republican activists in 1980.

Despite viewing Edward Kennedy as closer in ideology than Jimmy Carter, many liberal Democratic activists supported Carter; despite viewing George Bush as closer in ideology than Ronald Reagan, many moderate-to-liberal Republican activists supported Ronald Reagan. The question posed by these findings is what factor or set of factors overrode ideology in the choice of a presidential candidate? Perhaps rather than focusing solely on the immediate contest for their party's nomination, activists were also weighing the consequences of their decisions for the general election contest in November. If the delegates were concerned about the outcome of the November election as well as the nomination, their decisions may have been influenced by the candidates' prospects in that election in addition to ideology.

NOTES

1. See Appendix A for the specific wording of these questions. The response alternatives on the issue questions were

"strongly agree," "mildly agree," "neutral," "mildly disagree," and "strongly disagree."

2. The correlations (Pearson's r) between ideological self-placement and positions on 13 national issues ranged from .18 to .48 with an average of .34 for Democratic delegates and from .10 to .43 with an average of .23 for Republican delegates. The principal components factor analysis produced three factors with eigenvalues greater than one for Democratic delegates. However, the first factor accounted for 75 percent of the explained variance. The principal components analysis also produced three factors with eigenvalues greater than one for Republican delegates with the first factor accounting for 64 percent of the explained variance. Among Democratic delegates, only two issues loaded more strongly on the second or third factor than on the first factor. Among Republican delegates, only three issues loaded more strongly on the second or third factor than on the first factor.

3. Among Democratic delegates, 88 percent viewed Edward Kennedy as more liberal than Jimmy Carter while 5 percent viewed Carter as more liberal than Kennedy. Among Republican delegates, 80 percent viewed Ronald Reagan as more conservative than George Bush while 2 percent viewed Bush as more conservative than Reagan.

5

ELECTABILITY AND CANDIDATE CHOICE

Presidential activists want to win. This is the hypothesis of this chapter. The hypothesis may seem implausible in the face of the evidence in Chapter 3: activists say they would rather remain true to their ideological interests and lose than compromise their principles and win. Setting aside for a moment what activists say about their own motivations, is the hypothesis plausible? Politicians frequently use sports analogies in speaking of their craft, and anyone who has watched a football or basketball game knows the players (and the fans) want to win. Indeed, winning is the point, and it is only the relatively few "purists" who are more concerned with "how the game is played" than they are with the outcome. Political "games" like presidential nominations are much more important than the sports from which such metaphors are drawn. Is it reasonable to expect the players in the presidential nomination to care less than sports fans about winning?

We have seen that presidential activists are an ideological lot, although ideology is far from the perfect predictor of candidate preference that the purist model expects. Edward Kennedy, for example, did not receive the kind of support from his constituency in the liberal wing of the Democratic Party that the purist model leads us to expect. But an argument could be made that the more ideological activists are, and the more committed they are to issues like abortion or the environment, the more they will want to win. Even a moment's reflection should cause the typical activist to realize that promoting candidates who are less electable will only help the opposition party to gain victory. And the opposition party will often pursue issue and ideological outcomes diametrically opposed to those held so firmly by the activist!

If activists want to win, how can we explain the activists' own statements in Chapter 3 and in so many other studies to the contrary? We believe that general, abstract statements about "compromise" and "principles" tap values imbedded in the U.S. political culture and do not necessarily explain specific behaviors such as candidate support. Political parties, politics, and compromise are symbols that often have negative connotations to Americans, even to those actively involved in the process. Items such as those we reported in Chapter 3 may be tapping a general feeling that compromise "just to win" is not consistent with people's basic political values. It sounds tainted and smacks of unprincipled behavior. We shall demonstrate, however, that these general convictions—no doubt honestly held by our respondents and those studied in previous election years—do not predict candidate choice behavior.

In arguing that activists weigh electability very heavily in their candidate choice, we are stating that they anticipate the second, general election, stage of the process. This is precisely what the expected utility model of activists' candidate choice predicts. Moreover, to the extent that perceived electability is tied in activists' minds to congruence with popular preferences on an ideological dimension, we should expect activists concerned about electability to nominate candidates more in tune with the public's ideological preferences. In contrast, activists concerned primarily with nominating candidates consistent with their own ideological interests might choose nominees markedly out of line with the public's position.[1] Thus the theoretical import of electability as a central criterion of activists' nomination preferences is twofold: choosing electable candidates should help the parties maintain their strength as organizations by helping them choose viable candidates, and choosing electable candidates should result in nominees in line with the public's (but not necessarily party activists') policy preferences (cf. Page 1978).

These effects of an activist corps motivated by electability are directly related to the expected utility model. We begin our analysis of the model by focusing our attention on electability because so much of the survey literature denies its relevance. With our analysis of the effect of electability on candidate choice in hand we will be in a position to formulate and test an expected utility model in Chapter 6.

PERCEPTIONS OF CANDIDATE ELECTABILITY

Our focus upon candidate choice led us to develop candidate-specific estimates of electability similar to those used in Chapter 4 to measure ideological proximity. We asked activists in both parties to estimate the chances that each of six candidates would win the November election if that candidate were to receive the nomination of his party. Table 5.1 presents the perceived electability of each of the candidates. We also present the median score each candidate received in order to facilitate comparison (the lower the median electability score, the more electable the candidate was judged to be).

One of the most striking findings in Table 5.1 is that activists in both parties agreed on the relative electability of the contenders within each party. Democrats and Republicans alike saw Carter as the most electable candidate among the three Democratic contenders, followed by Kennedy and Brown. Likewise, activists in both parties agreed that Reagan was the strongest Republican followed by Bush and Anderson. To be sure, there is evidence of a partisan bias to the judgments that activists make about the six candidates. Democrats rated the candidates in their party as more electable than the Republicans did while Republicans saw Reagan and Bush (but not Anderson) as more electable in November than did the Democrats. Judging a candidate's electability is difficult and likely to be colored by the activist's partisan and ideological biases as well as the objective qualities that tend to make a candidate viable in a national election. But these partisan effects go only so far in affecting activists' perceptions. For example, Democrats on average rated Reagan as second only to Carter among all six candidates in his chances for a November victory, and they rated Bush as more likely to win than Brown. Republicans rated Reagan and Bush as strongest but did see Carter as more electable than Anderson.

Political choices always involve comparisons. We have focused most of our analysis upon the two major contenders within each party because they were the most visible and most viable candidates for their party's nomination. We shall continue this focus on the Carter-Kennedy race on the Democratic side, and the Reagan-Bush contest among the Republicans in our analysis of electability. We have created measures of the relative electability of the two major candidates in each party by combining activists' judgments about the electability of both candidates. The data from these relative measures presented in Table 5.2 are entirely consistent with our conclusions above. Carter was perceived as more electable than Kennedy by two-thirds of the activists in both parties. Reagan was judged to be more electable than Bush, especially among the Republicans. Only a small minority of activists perceived Kennedy or Bush

TABLE 5.1

Perceived Electability of Six Candidates by Activists in Both Parties

Democrats

If nominated:	Carter	Kennedy	Brown	Reagan	Bush	Anderson
Definitely would win	37%	10%	– %	6%	1%	2%
Probably would win	34	18	2	20	7	7
Might win	18	30	9	47	29	27
Probably would lose	8	25	32	17	39	33
Definitely would lose	4	17	57	11	25	31
Total	101%	100%	100%	100%	101%	100%
Median electability score	1.89	3.24	4.62	3.02	3.85	3.92
Weighted n =	9,404	8,772	8,300	7,618	7,396	7,500

Republicans

If nominated:	Carter	Kennedy	Brown	Reagan	Bush	Anderson
Definitely would win	2%	– %	– %	49%	8%	1%
Probably would win	11	2	–	36	28	3
Might win	42	11	2	12	35	17
Probably would lose	30	39	17	2	19	33
Definitely would lose	15	48	80	1	10	46
Total	100%	100%	99%	100%	100%	100%
Median electability score	3.38	4.44	4.88	1.53	2.90	4.36
Weighted n =	8,298	8,217	8,087	9,626	9,065	9,014

TABLE 5.2

Relative Electability of the Major Contenders in Each Party

	Democrats	Republicans
Carter more electable	67%	66%
Carter and Kennedy same	15	30
Kennedy more electable	18	5
Total	100%	101%
Weighted n =	8,637	8,132
Reagan more electable	55%	70%
Reagan and Bush same	34	22
Bush more electable	11	8
Total	100%	100%
Weighted n =	7,300	9,010

as more likely to win the election if they received their party's nomination.

That the Democrats and Republicans rated Carter as stronger than Kennedy is not surprising. Carter was the incumbent president with all the advantages that implies. He was reasonably skillful in exploiting the presidency to his electoral benefit particularly during the early months of the Kennedy challenge when Carter pleaded the Iranian crisis had to be his top priority. Moreover, Carter was perceived to be closer to the center than Kennedy among Democrats (70 percent thought Carter was closer to the center while only 8 percent saw Kennedy as more moderate than Carter) and Republicans alike (63 percent saw Carter as more centrist while only 1 percent of the Republicans saw Kennedy as closer to the center).[2] Thus activists in both parties seemed to conform to the conventional wisdom that an incumbent and a relative moderate was likely to be the stronger November candidate, at least in their judgments about the two Democratic contestants.

As our analysis thus far makes clear, activists in both parties rejected the notion that extremists make weak general election candidates in their judgments about the relative electability of the Republican contenders. We have already seen in Chapter 4 that activists perceived Ronald Reagan as relatively extreme on our liberal-conservative continuum. And there was little doubt in the minds of our respondents that Bush was the more moderate candidate: 71 percent of the Republicans and 66 percent of the Democrats perceived Bush as closer to the ideological center while less than 4 percent in either party saw Reagan as more moderate. The lessons of Anthony Downs (1957) and the elections of 1964 and 1972 notwithstanding, activists may have discounted Reagan's extremism in concluding that he was the strongest Republican candidate, deciding that his other virtues outweighed the fact that he might be ideologically out of line with much of the voting public. His visibility from previous campaigns and his acknowledged mastery of television communications were evidently judged important to Reagan's November chances.

The relative electability of the candidates was due in part to factors visible to most observers of the 1980 campaign. Nonetheless, there was enough variation in activists' perceptions of the candidate's electability to merit further investigation. Certainly the fact that activists in both political parties eschewed conventional wisdom and saw Reagan as more electable than the moderate George Bush should be explored. Finally, because candidate electability is such an important part of our explanation of activists' candidate choice, we seek to explain as fully as the data will permit variation in perceived electability.

Having noted that activists were generally convinced Reagan was the most electable Republican candidate despite his relatively extreme brand of conservatism, can we nonetheless find some variation in perceived electability consistent with the hypothesis that relative proximity to the center of the ideological spectrum affects perceived electability? Table 5.3 presents evidence on this question. Democrats accepted the conventional wisdom only to a limited degree. Among the relatively few Democrats who saw Kennedy as more centrist than Carter, a majority still thought Carter was more electable. Nonetheless, there is a weak relationship between perceived electability and relative proximity to the center. Only 13 percent of the Democrats who saw Carter as the more centrist candidate thought Kennedy was more electable in November while 37 percent of those who thought Kennedy was more centrist perceived the Massachusetts senator as more electable. A similar, though slightly weaker relationship, exists among the Republicans. They tended to think Carter was the stronger candidate regardless of which candidate they saw as more centrist, though there was some effect of proximity to the center. Thus activists in both parties judged Carter to be more electable than Kennedy, but not primarily because he was the more centrist candidate. Indeed,

TABLE 5.3

Relationship between Candidate Proximity to the Center and Electability

		Democrats						
		Candidate Closer to the Center				Candidate Closer to the Center		
		Carter	Same	Kennedy		Reagan	Same	Bush
Candidate more electable	Carter	72%	52%	55%	Reagan	78%	57%	52%
	Same	15	20	8	Same	14	36	34
	Kennedy	13	29	37	Bush	8	7	15
Total		100%	101%	100%		100%	100%	101%
Weighted n =		5,551	1,746	633		210	1,953	4,328
		Republicans						
		Carter	Same	Kennedy		Reagan	Same	Bush
Candidate more electable	Carter	71%	57%	52%	Reagan	82%	70%	70%
	Same	25	38	35	Same	11	26	21
	Kennedy	4	5	13	Bush	7	4	9
Total		100%	100%	100%		100%	100%	100%
Weighted n =		4,915	2,622	107		319	2,202	6,113

had a Democratic contender appeared in 1980 who was not an ideological moderate, but who appeared on other grounds to be very strong, the data in Table 5.3 suggest the Democrats would have had no hesitation granting him the nomination.

This, of course, is exactly what the Republicans did in nominating Ronald Reagan. Table 5.3 demonstrates that Republicans were only very weakly influenced in their judgments of Reagan's electability by their perceptions of his proximity to the center. Similarly, Democrats were willing to grant that Reagan was stronger than Bush, with only a weak effect of relative ideological extremism. Thus activists in both parties were remarkably consistent in viewing the effects of candidates' ideology on their electability. A candidate with other electoral resources in easily superior, in their view, to a candidate who is merely moderate. Perhaps activists were not impressed with the ideological character of the U.S. electorate, preferring to believe instead that factors such as visibility, incumbency, and style were more important in determining a candidate's chances in November.

If the ideological position of the candidate does not have a particularly strong influence on activists' perceptions of candidate electability, it still may be the case that ideology colors judgments of electability by causing activists to see their ideological favorite as more electable. We have seen in various ways in Chapters 3 and 4 that the activists we surveyed are ideological, hold strong beliefs on the issues. Moreover, we have seen that activists tended to adopt a "purist" orientation toward the electability-ideology tradeoff when questioned about the desirability of compromise in order to nominate a winner. One way of avoiding decisional conflict associated with possible tension between ideological preferences and perceived electability is to rationalize that the candidate who is preferred on ideological grounds is also the most electable.

Table 5.4 presents data supporting the hypothesis that activists tended to rationalize their strongly held ideological preferences in reaching judgments about candidate electability. While an overwhelming majority of Democrats ideologically closer to Carter saw him as more electable, only 44 percent of those ideologically closer to Kennedy judged the president to be more electable than his principal challenger. An almost identical pattern is evident among the Republicans.

Despite the evidence of rationalization, the relative strength of the candidates is clearly and consistently reflected in Table 5.4. For one thing, among activists equally proximate to both candidates on the ideological scale, Carter and Reagan were

TABLE 5.4

Activists' Ideological Proximity and Perceived Candidate Electability

		Democrats Ideologically Closer to:		
		Carter	No Differ- ence	Kennedy
Candidate more	Carter	86%	71%	44%
electable	Same	8	16	22
	Kennedy	6	12	34
Total		100%	99%	100%
Weighted n =		3,342	1,207	3,122

		Republicans Ideologically Closer to:		
		Reagan	No Differ- ence	Bush
Candidate more	Reagan	88%	61%	46%
electable	Same	11	31	35
	Bush	2	7	19
Total		101%	100%	100%
Weighted n =		4,169	2,049	2,266

perceived to be most electable by Democratic and Republican activists respectively. More importantly, only one-third of the Democrats closer to Kennedy perceived Kennedy as more electable than Carter while less than one-fifth of George Bush's ideological compatriots within the Republican party managed to view him as more electable than Ronald Reagan. Thus the covariation between ideological preferences and electability is definitely bounded by the relative electoral strengths of the contenders within each party.

We have seen that activists' judgments about candidate electability are colored by their ideological preferences and, to a much lesser degree, by their perceptions of how close to the ideological center the candidate is. We also saw in Table 5.1 that perceptions of candidate electability were influenced by partisanship. In Table 5.5 we report a regression analysis of the electability of the two major candidates in each party that permits us to see the relative effect of partisanship, ideological proximity, and centrism.[3] The standardized regression coefficients show a consistent pattern: party identification has a much stronger effect on perceived electability than does ideological proximity. And with these two variables controlled, the effects of our measure of centrism dwindle to near insignificance, both statistically and substantively. That partisanship affects perceived electability more than ideological proximity is an important finding. First, it is not unexpected: we have known for some time that party identification is an important perceptual screen for voters as they sort out their perceptions of political leaders and issues (Campbell et al. 1960). More to the point, however, the strong partisan bias as Democrats judge the electability of Republican candidates, and as Republicans weigh the strength of Democratic contenders, is not particularly relevant to what we view as primarily an intraparty choice. Partisan activists can protect themselves from dissonance by viewing the opposition's candidates as generally weaker than their own and thus commit themselves wholeheartedly to the task of nominating and electing their party's candidates. Thus this sort of perceptual bias ultimately works to the good of the political parties.

But severe bias within the parties is potentially troubling as we seek to understand the process of activist candidate choice.

TABLE 5.5

Predictors of Candidate Electability

	Candidate			
	Carter	Kennedy	Reagan	Bush
Party identification	.617	.402	-.529	-.542
Intraparty relative ideological proximity	.273	-.298	.180	-.321
Intraparty relative proximity to the center	.014*	.040	-.021	.034
$R^2 =$	.344	.324	.399	.233

*Not significant at the .05 level.

Note: Coefficients are standardized regression coefficients. Unweighted n = 12,283.

If activists rationalize their judgments of electability from their ideological preferences, it will be difficult to argue electability has an independent effect on candidate choice. Moreover, if rationalization is prevalent among activists, that is entirely consistent with the view that activists are purists interested primarily in advancing their own ideological preferences even if that means losing the election. Rationalizing activists, of course, would fail to see a problem simply because they would see their ideological favorite as also most electable.[4] Despite the fact that the ideology bias is not as strong as the partisan bias in Table 5.5, it is important enough so that we must take it fully into account as we weigh the effects of ideology and electability on candidate choice.

ELECTABILITY AND CANDIDATE CHOICE

We have said we believe activists want to win. If this is the case, their preferences for their party's nomination should be strongly influenced by their judgments about candidate electability. The simple relationship between perceived candidate electability and candidate preference depicted in Table 5.6 strongly supports our contention. Among Democrats judging Carter to be more electable than Kennedy, fully 93 percent preferred the incumbent president, while those who saw Kennedy as more electable supported the Massachusetts challenger by an even larger majority. Likewise, Republicans seeing Reagan as more electable than his principal challenger preferred him over Bush by a margin of 94 to 6 percent. The small minority of Republican activists who thought Bush more likely to win the November election if he were to receive the GOP nomination chose Bush overwhelmingly.

A quick comparison of Table 5.6 to Table 4.7 confirms the hypothesis that 1980 presidential activists' candidate preferences were more strongly influenced by electability than they were by personal ideological inclinations. Table 4.7 showed that Kennedy and Bush both failed to capture their "share" of their own ideological constituencies as both challengers experienced substantial defections by activists who perceived themselves to be ideologically closer to them than to their party's front-runner. George Bush was especially unfortunate in this respect because he actually lost a majority of Republican activists closer ideologically to him than to Governor Reagan. In contrast, Table 5.6 shows that both challengers did extremely well among activists who perceived them to be stronger candidates in the general election. Indeed,

TABLE 5.6

Candidate Preference by Perceived Electability

More Electable Candidate

		Democrats		
		Carter More Electable	Both Equally Electable	Kennedy More Electable
Candidate	Carter	93%	33%	3%
preference	Kennedy	7	67	97
Total		100%	100%	100%
Weighted n =		4,963	874	1,339

		Republicans		
		Reagan More Electable	Both Equally Electable	Bush More Electable
Candidate	Reagan	94%	51%	5%
preference	Bush	6	49	95
Total		100%	100%	100%
Weighted n =		5,133	1,350	508

it apparently was the comparative electability advantage Carter and Reagan enjoyed in the minds of activists that accounts for their nominations rather than the success of their ideological appeals.

ELECTABILITY VERSUS IDEOLOGY AND ISSUES

Our contention that electability was a more important influence on activists' candidate choice demands substantiation, particularly in light of the overwhelmingly "purist" orientation of our respondents reported in Chapter 3. When we combine our measures of ideological proximity and electability, we can readily see that electability was considerably more powerful an influence on candidate preference than was ideological proximity (see Table 5.7). Regardless of which candidate activists found more ideologically compatible, they tended to support the candi-

TABLE 5.7

Candidate Preference by Perceived Electability and Ideological Proximity

More Electable Candidate

	Democrats		
	Carter More Electable	Both Equally Electable	Kennedy More Electable
Closer to Carter	98 (n = 2,180)	57 (n = 148)	7 (n = 128)
Equal distance	94 (n = 643)	57 (n = 106)	4 (n = 91
Closer to Kennedy	78 (n = 921)	18 (n = 409)	2 (n = 760)

	Republicans		
	Reagan More Electable	Both Equally Electable	Bush More Electable
Closer to Reagan	99 (n = 2,348)	75 (n = 257)	24 (n = 34)
Equal distance	91 (n = 776)	60 (n = 324)	8 (n = 76)
Closer to Bush	83 (n = 586)	29 (n = 422)	2 (n = 217)

Note: Entries are percentages of Democratic delegates supporting Carter and percentages of Republican delegates supporting Reagan. N shown is actual number of cases. Percentages based on weighted n.

date they saw as more electable. Among Democrats closer ideologically to Kennedy, but who thought Carter was more likely to win in November, fully 78 percent supported Carter for the nomination. Similarly, 83 percent of the Republicans closer to Bush, but who viewed Reagan as more electable, gave their support to Reagan. On the other side, of the Democratic activists closer to Carter, but who thought Kennedy was more

electable, only 7 percent supported the president (and 93 percent gave their support to Kennedy). Reagan did a little better
among those who were ideologically closer to him but who thought
Bush was more electable, as 24 percent chose him over Bush.
Ideological proximity had a marked impact on candidate preference only among the minority of activists who saw no difference
between the candidates' chances for a November victory. The
overriding importance of electability in determining candidate
preference is evident in these results and directly contradicts
the impression that these activists tended to be ideological purists
with little interest in compromising their ideological interests to
win the November election.

Table 5.8 provides a detailed breakdown of the bases of
the candidate support decision for our respondents. Using
candidate electability and ideological proximity, we have cate-
gorized activists according to whether these two variables re-
inforced one another, whether there was tension between ideology
and electability, and whether they were indifferent on either
ideology or electability.[5] In both parties, the largest proportion
of activists experienced no decisional conflict between ideology
and electability. Fifty-four percent of the Democrats and 49
percent of the Republicans supported a candidate whom they
believed to be both more electable and closer ideologically to
their own preferences than the other major contender for the
party's nomination. Among those who experienced tension between ideology and electability, the overwhelming majority of
activists in both parties chose the candidate whom they believed
to be more electable, sacrificing their ideological interests.
Seventy-nine percent of the Democrats who saw their ideological
favorite as less electable than his contender supported the more
electable candidate while 85 percent of the Republicans experiencing tension went with electability and against their ideological
inclinations. Among those seeing no difference between the
ideological proximity of the two contenders in their party, 93
percent of the Democrats and 94 percent of the Republicans
supported the candidate judged more electable.

Interesting differences between the candidate factions in
each party are visible. The earlier literature using general
measures of "amateurism" or "purism" found that style differences
among activists were at least moderately associated with candidate
preference (for example, Soule and Clarke 1970; Soule and
McGrath 1975; Roback 1980). Using our purism-pragmatism
measures in Chapter 3, we reported weak associations in 1980.
Purists in the Democratic Party tended to favor Senator Kennedy
more than pragmatists although a majority of purists still favored

TABLE 5.8

Base of Candidate Support by Party and Candidate Preference

	All Democrats	Carter Supporters	Kennedy Supporters	All Republicans	Reagan Supporters	Bush Supporters
Ideology and electability reinforced	54%	58%	44%	49%	56%	22%
Tension between ideology and electability:						
Chose with electability	15	19	8	11	13	3
Chose with ideology	4	0*	12	2	0*	10
Indifferent on ideology, chose with electability	13	16	5	16	18	8
Indifferent on electability chose with ideology	8	2	20	9	5	28
Unaccounted for	6	4	11	12	8	29
Total	100%	99%	100%	99%	100%	100%
Weighted n =	6,421	4,388	2,033	6,559	5,221	1,333

*Weighted n = 12 for the Carter Democrats, and 11 for the Reagan Republicans.

President Carter. On the Republican side, purists were more likely to prefer Reagan over Bush although, again, Reagan was the run-away favorite among both purists and pragmatists. Thus our Chapter 3 findings were consistent with the findings of past studies: purists tend to favor the candidate generally perceived as more extreme while pragmatists tend to favor the more moderate candidate. The data in Table 5.8 only partially support this finding. Jimmy Carter, who ran a campaign that emphasized in various ways his electability, drew a healthy proportion of his support from those who clearly sought to nominate a winner. Virtually 100 percent of those supporting him who saw a conflict between their interest in nominating a winner and their ideology apparently supported him because he was more electable than Kennedy. If we include those equally proximate to Carter and Kennedy, 35 percent of Carter's support came to him because he was judged the more electable of the two major contenders.

Perhaps because Kennedy's challenge emphasized his traditional Democratic liberalism against Carter's relative conservatism, more of the Senator's support can be linked to ideology. Indeed, among those experiencing direct conflict between electability and ideology, a majority (61 percent) based their support for Kennedy on their ideological interests and against their judgment that Carter was the stronger November candidate. If we include those indifferent on electability or ideology, a total of 31 percent of the Kennedy faction acted out of their ideological interest while only 12 percent backed him because of an interest in winning. In terms of the electability-ideology tradeoff, therefore, Kennedy's support was more "purist" than the president's even though, overall, Democratic activists tended to back the candidate they viewed as more electable.

The Democratic results in Table 5.8 are not particularly surprising because Kennedy was relatively extreme and because our Chapter 3 analysis showed purists to be more favorable to his candidacy than pragmatists. But on the Republican side, the conventional wisdom (along with our earlier results from the "purism-pragmatism" index) that relatively extreme candidates will be more likely to attract ideologically based support is refuted. Among the supporters of Ronald Reagan who experienced tension between their ideological preferences and electability, virtually 100 percent ignored their ideological preference for Bush and supported Reagan. If we include those indifferent between Reagan and Bush on ideological or electability grounds, nearly one-third (31 percent) of Reagan's support was based on the fact that he was the more electable candidate whereas only 5 percent of his support resulted from activists choosing him for ideological reasons. Ronald Reagan, the candidate that activists in both parties judged to be more ideological, attracted a significant portion of his support from activists concerned primarily about nominating a winner.

George Bush, in contrast, was viewed as overwhelmingly the more centrist of the two serious Republican contenders, yet his support was linked much more to ideological preferences. Among his supporters feeling tension, only 23 percent supported him because they viewed him as more electable while 77 percent ignored their judgment that Reagan was more electable and chose Bush out of their interest in maximizing their ideological concerns. Likewise, only 8 percent of his total support came from those equally proximate to both Bush and Reagan but who selected Bush because they saw him as more electable. Almost one-fourth (23 percent) of the Bush supporters saw Reagan and Bush as equally electable and supported Bush because of ideology. In total, 38 percent of the Bush faction supported him out of an ideological affinity—a larger proportion than supported Senator Kennedy for the same reason (32 percent) and far more than supported Reagan or Carter out of ideological interests (5 and 3 percent respectively).

In short, the evidence in Tables 5.7 and 5.8 shows a real concern among activists in both parties with choosing the candidate most likely to win the November election. Because they were viewed as most likely to win, Carter and Reagan were the runaway favorites among the activists we surveyed in 1980. Differences among candidate factions are evident in the data, but these differences do not necessarily confirm the conventional wisdom. Teddy Kennedy did attract a significant proportion of his support from those who agreed with him ideologically, a finding consistent with earlier studies showing ideologically "extreme" candidates to be more likely to attract "purist" support. In marked contrast to that hypothesis, however, George Bush's moderate drive for the GOP nomination attracted the largest share of "purist" supporters among all four candidates. That he was able to gather only about 20 percent of the Republican activists into his camp is probably due to the fact that he was judged less likely to win among so many Republican activists committed to nominating a winner. Finally, note that a large proportion of activists in both parties were blissfully free of tension between their interests in ideology and electability. We return to the implications of this finding after an analysis of specific issues.

ISSUES, IDEOLOGY, AND ELECTABILITY

We have shown in Chapter 4 that issues had a significant impact on 1980 candidate choice in both parties. On the Democratic side, Senator Kennedy's challenge to President Carter was tied to specific issues like national health insurance, draft registration, and wage-price controls. On the Republican side, issues like the ERA, abortion, and defense spending tended to be most divisive (see Tables 4.4 and 4.5). Presidential activists are an ideological group, and many of their specific issue preferences can be expected to fit into a relatively well-developed belief system organized along the liberal-conservative dimension. To the extent that this is true, our analysis of ideological proximity and electability presented thus far should present an accurate picture depicting, as it does, electability as more important than ideology.

But many have correctly pointed out that special interest concerns have become increasingly important in U.S. national politics. Critics of the contemporary presidential election process do not hesitate to apply this observation to presidential nominations, suggesting that presidential activists may be motivated by special interests to the exclusion of other considerations such as electability and party unity. In a relatively open process, candidates for the nomination may garner support by appealing to fairly isolated special interests such as those intensely concerned about emotional issues like the draft, environment, or abortion. To the extent that the contemporary process draws activists motivated by these kinds of special interests into the fray, the general ideological dimension may be a misrepresentation of their issue concerns, and our analysis thus far may overstate the importance of electability.

Table 5.9 presents a discriminant analysis of candidate choice in both parties, examining the relative effects of electability, ideological proximity, and the 13 issues we included in our survey. In both parties, the effect of electability remains far and away the strongest, even with ideological proximity and the issues included in the analysis. This strongly supports our contention that activists in 1980 wanted to win. The effect of electability is slightly greater on the Democratic side than among Republicans, consistent with our earlier findings showing Bush Republicans to be relatively more concerned with ideology. Indeed, among the Democrats it is difficult to find any effects of specific issues. The strongest effects are linked to the re-institution of draft registration, wage-price controls, and national health insurance. These were all issues that sharply divided

TABLE 5.9

Discriminant Analysis of the Effects of Electability, Ideology, and Issue Opinion on Candidate Choice

	Democrats (n = 4,302)	Republicans (n = 4,226)
Perceived relative electability	.747	.632
Ideological proximity	.322	.252
Equal Rights Amendment	.022	-.310
Antiabortion amendment	.007	.157
Increase defense spending	-.066	.137
National health insurance	-.113	.080
Develop nuclear power	.047	.024
Cut nondefense spending	.003	.040
Affirmative action	.044	-.009
Deregulate oil	.051	.091
Wage-Price Controls	-.142	.045
Reduce inflation/increase unemployment	.036	-.063
Reinstitution of the draft	.192	.006
SALT II	.075	.099
Increase U.S. military in Middle East	.017	.098
Canonical correlation	.776	.594

President Carter from Kennedy. Carter had taken the initiative in reinstituting draft registration in response to heightened tensions between the United States and the Soviet Union, a move strongly opposed by Kennedy and by many Democrats still smarting from the political effects of Vietnam. Kennedy argued that the nation needed a comprehensive health insurance plan—a policy initiative that he vigorously promoted in the Senate—and that the nation's economic difficulties demanded strong federal (and presidential) remedy. On both issues he charged that the president was more like a Republican than a Democrat and that he should therefore be denied the nomination. Despite the divisive character of these issues for the candidates, Democratic activists were not particularly influenced by them in their candidate choice, nor did these issues appear to interfere with their enthusiasm for nominating a winner.

Whereas the issues that divided the Democratic contestants in 1980 could arguably be seen as fitting fairly neatly into the traditional liberal-conservative framework, the issues that most separated the Reagan and Bush camps could be viewed as less relevant to the usual ideological symbols. The two highest ranking issues in Table 5.9 among Republicans are the Equal Rights Amendment (ERA) and abortion. On both issues, Bush and Reagan were fairly clearly differentiated, particularly because Ronald Reagan did not hesitate to display his "new right" credentials. He consistently expressed his opposition to the Equal Rights Amendment (while voicing support for equal rights for women), and he actively supported an amendment to the Constitution prohibiting abortions. These two issues excited considerable emotion on both sides, and the ERA issue had a greater effect on candidate choice than ideological proximity. Even this issue, however, does not approach electability in its effect, and the next most powerful issue is even less important than ideology. The effects of the several defense-related issues remain quite small despite the fact that Bush adopted a noticeably less belligerent stand on these issues toward the Soviet Union than did Ronald Reagan. That issues like cutting nondefense spending in order to balance the budget did not have a greater effect on Republicans' candidate preference after George Bush's charges that Reagan's proposals constituted a "voodoo economics" is remarkable.

Part of the concern of those worried about special interests dominating presidential nominations relates to the intensity with which some issue opinions are held. Strongly held beliefs, rather than merely favoring one side of the issue or the other, may indeed interfere with activists' interest in electability, even if the number of such strongly committed activists constitutes a minority. In order to test this possibility, we present in Table 5.10 the relationship between electability and candidate choice among Democrats expressing strong opposition or support for the issues. We have included the five issues that had the greatest independent impact on candidate preference according to the discriminant analysis in Table 5.9.

Even with an issue such as the draft that has the potential of exciting considerable emotion and thus might stimulate a purist attitude toward compromise, the effect of electability remains remarkably strong among the Democratic activists. Among those strongly opposed to reinstituting the draft but who thought Carter the stronger candidate, 74 percent supported Carter over Kennedy thus acting against their deeply held opinion. Likewise, on the economic and defense issues that

TABLE 5.10

Percent Democrats Supporting Carter by Electability and Opinion on Selected Issues

Issue Opinion

Issue	Strongly Favor			Strongly Oppose		
	Carter More Electable	Same	Kennedy More Electable	Carter More Electable	Same	Kennedy More Electable
Reinstitution of draft registration	97 (1,464)	46 (108)	5 (182)	74 (440)	17 (266)	2 (532)
Wage-price controls	83 (590)	20 (168)	4 (470)	97 (915)	53 (57)	8 (87)
National health insurance	83 (841)	25 (353)	2 (670)	99 (711)	65 (29)	14 (28)
SALT II	91 (755)	29 (187)	2 (301)	92 (440)	34 (55)	8 (121)
Increase defense spending/decrease domestic	97 (1,073)	49 (66)	6 (129)	87 (559)	20 (282)	2 (466)

Note: Cell entries are percent supporting Carter. Weighted n's are in parentheses.

divided the candidates, activists were consistently willing to ignore their strongly held beliefs in order to support the candidate they saw as more electable. Issue opinion does have an effect on candidate choice, especially among activists who saw no difference between Carter and Kennedy in their electability, but electability is obviously of overriding importance to the Democratic activists.[6]

Analysis of the five issues that had the greatest impact on the discriminant analysis of Republican candidate choice shows a pattern very similar to what we have seen for the Democrats. Table 5.11 demonstrates that highly emotional issues like the ERA and abortion did not deter Republican activists from selecting the candidate they saw as most electable. Among the minority of Republican activists strongly favoring the Equal Rights Amendment and perceiving Reagan as more electable than Bush, for example, 76 percent still supported Reagan. Eighty-eight percent of the Republicans strongly opposed to an antiabortion amendment, but who saw Reagan as the more electable November candidate, gave him their support. Once again, therefore, we find activists strongly committed to an issue, yet willing to compromise their position on that issue in order to help nominate a winner. Across the five issues included in Table 5.11 (and the others not included in the table), the effect of electability is monotonously strong whether the issue related to the differences between Reagan and Bush on social issues, the economy, or national defense, and regardless of how intensely the opinion was held. Republican presidential activists, like their Democratic counterparts, were concerned far more with nominating a candidate whom they believed had the best chance of winning the November election than they were with protecting their personal (and sometimes intensely held) issue opinions.

We have found that our analysis of specific issues—even highly emotional issues that divided the candidates within each party rather sharply—does not undermine our thesis that activists in 1980 wanted to win. In contrast to the purist model, and in contradiction to activists' own self-assessments reported in Chapter 3, activists appear to be substantially less concerned with maximizing their ideological or issue concerns than they are with winning. Before we conclude that the purist model of activists' candidate choice is incorrect, however, one final caveat must be considered. In our analysis of electability, we showed that activists' perceptions of electability were related to their ideological preferences. Thus an activist ideologically predisposed toward Kennedy might be inclined to judge him more electable than Carter as a way of protecting himself from the

TABLE 5.11

Percent Republicans Supporting Reagan by Electability and Opinion on Selected Issues

	Issue Opinion					
	Strongly Favor			Strongly Oppose		
Issue	Reagan More Electable	Same	Bush More Electable	Reagan More Electable	Same	Bush More Electable
Equal Rights Amendment	76 (272)	24 (207)	0 (126)	98 (2,719)	72 (374)	11 (71)
Antiabortion amendment	98 (1,832)	67 (201)	10 (53)	88 (969)	42 (436)	3 (224)
Increase defense spending/decrease domestic	97 (3,338)	65 (627)	6 (171)	78 (54)	22 (5)	0 (6)
SALT II	89 (109)	38 (28)	5 (11)	97 (3,089)	64 (631)	11 (145)
Increase military presence in the Middle East	97 (1,475)	66 (260)	4 (70)	90 (166)	58 (22)	23 (20)

Note: Cell entries are percent supporting Reagan. Weighted n's are in parentheses.

dissonance that would arise from perceived tension between
electability and ideology. Indeed we saw from Table 5.8 that
a majority of Democrats and a near majority of Republicans
experienced no tension between electability and ideology since
their favored candidate was in their minds both more electable
and ideologically closer than his competitor. If this congruence
resulted from activists rationalizing that their ideologically
favored candidate was more electable, the purist thesis would
be saved even though our analysis thus far shows electability
to be stronger when there is tension. The total weight of
electability on candidate choice would be swamped by ideology
if all the congruence resulted from ideology affecting perceived
candidate electability.

We shall employ path analysis to test for the total effect
of ideology and electability on candidate choice.[7] And because
we have found issues to have some independent effect on choice,
we include an issue index in our analysis.[8] With the issue index,
the argument is parallel to that for ideological proximity: an
activist's positions on the issues could also cause him to see
the candidate most consistent with his positions to be the most
electable. For this analysis, we assume that all the relationship
between ideology and electability results from activists rationalizing their ideological preferences. Certainly part of the
relationship results from a reverse process whereby activists
rationalized their ideological and issue preferences because
they sought balance with their judgments about which candidates
were most electable. But our assumption allows us to conduct
a very conservative test of our thesis that electability is the
most important influence on candidate choice.

The analysis in Figure 5.1 shows that both ideological
proximity and the issue index had some effect on activists'
perceptions of candidate electability, but the results in the
upper half of the figure also show that electability had far and
away the greatest direct effect on candidate choice. These
findings are entirely consistent with results we have already
reported. The compound path analysis in the lower half of the
figure permits us to see that in both parties the direct effect
of electability on candidate choice easily outweighs the total
effect of either ideology or issues. Indeed, even if we combine
the total effects of ideology and issues in each party, the total
effect of electability still remains stronger.

These results provide powerful evidence in support of our
contention that presidential activists want to win. If we were
to acknowledge that judgments about electability may also affect
perceived ideological proximity, the relative effect of electability

FIGURE 5.1

A Path Analysis of the Rationalization Hypothesis

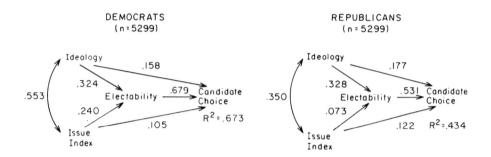

COMPOUND PATH ANALYSIS

	DEMOCRATS			REPUBLICANS		
	Electability	Ideology	Issues	Electability	Ideology	Issues
Direct Effect	.679	.158	.105	.531	.177	.122
Indirect Effect	-	.220	.163	-	.174	.039
Total Effect	.679	.378	.268	.531	.351	.161

Note: All Coefficients are Standardized Regression, or Path, Coefficients.
Weighted Ns Reported.

would increase. However, even the model most compatible with the purist hypothesis cannot prevent the conclusion that presidential activists in 1980 were more influenced by their desire to nominate a winner than they were by their ideological and issue interests.

CONCLUSIONS

If activists want to win, we should be able to find evidence that a candidate's electability influences their decision about whom to support for their party's nomination. Conversely, if activists really are ideological purists (as they say they are), we should be able to show that ideology is the most important influence on their candidate choice behavior. We have shown in this chapter that activists are influenced more by electability than they are by ideological proximity. Where there is a direct conflict between ideology and electability, most activists support the candidate they view as more electable. Even if we assume that all of the overlap between activists' judgments about which candidates are ideologically closer to them and which candidates are most electable results from activists rationalizing their ideological preferences, electability still turns out to be the most important influence. In addition, we could find no evidence that special interests—even on issues where emotions are likely to run deep—interfere with activists' desire to nominate a winner. So, activists want to win. This is an important conclusion because it relates to the health of the political parties in a period when many view U.S. party organizations to be in serious trouble. The single most important function of the national parties is the nomination of candidates for the presidency. If they perform this function "badly"—that is, if they nominate candidates who for various reasons are not likely to win the general election—they may hasten their own demise. This last statement is a loaded one. It suggests that "good" parties nominate candidates likely to win whereas "bad" parties nominate candidates who will lose. We delay discussion of most of the implications of this statement until the conclusion, after we have presented a full-blown model of activist candidate choice. But we can note here that we think on balance the parties perform useful functions in U.S. politics and that anything that they do, or that is done to them, that seriously weakens them is probably bad for U.S. democratic politics. The question is a complex one that involves more than just winning and losing. For example, we also think there is great merit to the argument that the parties ought to provide significant programmatic choice. And the two goals—winning and programmatic choice—may not be incompatible.

Our conclusion that presidential activists want to win (and therefore do not perform the nominating function "badly" at all) should not be interpreted as meaning issues and ideology play no role. We have shown that the activists we surveyed are an ideological lot and even that ideological concerns weigh heavily in their candidate choice support. Our purpose in this chapter has been to show that electability counts and counts heavily, not that ideology is irrelevant. Our expected utility model of candidate support will show that activists quite rationally temper their ideological interests with a reasonably sophisticated appraisal of what is likely to happen in the general election. In short, they realize politics is compromising one's ideals to get what one can, rather than pursuing ideals for their own sake.

NOTES

1. A large number of studies have shown that party activists are ideologically unrepresentative of partisan identifiers in the general public. For examples, see Farah, Jennings, and Miller (1981); Jackson, Brown, and Bositis (1982); and McClosky, Hoffman, and O'Hara (1960).

2. Our measure of relative centrism is simply a comparison of each candidate's absolute distance from the center of our liberal-conservative scale (coded "3" on our five-point scale).

3. We analyze the electability of each candidate separately in order to observe the effects of partisanship. The relative electability of each candidate within a party is only weakly affected by partisanship.

4. This assumes that all the association between ideology and electability results from activists rationalizing their ideological preferences in reaching judgments about candidate electability. We make this assumption below in order to subject our analysis to the most conservative possible test (see Figure 5.1).

5. Activists who support a candidate when they are indifferent on both ideology and electability, or who are indifferent on one variable but do not select the candidate consistent with the other, are "unaccounted for" in Table 5.8.

6. An examination of the relationship between electability and candidate choice for each of the five categories of intensity of issue opinion ("strongly favor," "favor," "undecided," "oppose," and "strongly oppose") for the issues in Table 5.10 reveals a gamma correlation of no less than .94 between electability and candidate choice.

7. Despite the fact that the dependent variable is dichotomous, we perform a path analysis using ordinary least squares (OLS) because it is the most straightforward technique for assessing the relative causal effects (both direct and indirect) of the independent variables. Gillespie (1977) compares OLS with log-linear techniques when the dependent variable is dichotomous and argues that while log-linear methods correct for some of the statistical problems associated with using OLS in this situation, these techniques do not permit the researcher to decompose the causal effects as we wish to do. On balance, the statistical limitations of OLS appear to be offset by its considerable benefits in this application.

8. The issue index is a simple additive one composed of all 13 issue items. See Appendix A for the wording of the issue questions. Before creating the index, the items were recoded to a consistent liberal-conservative direction.

6

AN EXPECTED UTILITY THEORY
OF CANDIDATE CHOICE

> The art of politics is the art of compromise. If I
> can get a whole loaf, I'll take it. If not, I'll take
> half rather than lose it all.
>> —Delegate to the Republican national conven-
>> tion, 1964 (Wildavsky 1965, p. 395)

Having demonstrated that activists want to win, our task
now is to come to a more coherent theoretical understanding of
how activists decide whom to support for their party's nomination. We might conclude from the last chapter that activists
simply look over the contenders, decide which candidate has
the best chance of winning the White House, and support that
candidate. Such a model would appear to explain a large proportion of activists' choices. Our purpose in Chapter 5 was to
argue that winning is a critical—even the single most important—
factor in determining candidate preference. But, perhaps
unlike professional football, winning in politics is not everything.
People become active in presidential politics because they want
to affect public policy. We have argued that the purist model
overemphasizes the issue and ideological motivations of activists,
but we do not want to be read as saying these things are of no
import.

The rational choice model begins with the assumption that
presidential activists are rational actors. That is, they participate in presidential nomination campaigns in order to promote
outcomes consistent with their perceived self-interest. The
model also assumes that the two-state character of the process
influences the way in which activists decide in the first stage.
These assumptions lead us to formulate an expected utility model
of candidate choice. Such a model permits us to acknowledge
that activists want to affect public policy (that is, they have

ideological interests) and that they want to win. Indeed, winning is instrumental to the goal of influencing public policy. Their participation in the nomination process will reflect these two goals. Moreover, the model will permit us to recognize that there will sometimes be tension between the goals of maximizing ideological goals and promoting the most electable candidate, and it suggests a way which the rational activist will resolve the tension. We will show that an expected utility model of candidate support does a better job of predicting nomination choice than either electability or ideology alone.

Briefly, the idea is that activists weigh the utility they will receive from each contender's nomination and the chances that the contender will actually win the election (and thus be able to deliver the utility to the activist). A Democratic activist in 1980, therefore, might compare the policy utility that he would receive from a Carter and a Kennedy candidacy. On balance, he might agree with more of Kennedy's policy positions and as a result determine that he would receive more "utility" (be happier, be more satisfied with public policy) from a Kennedy presidency than from another Carter presidency. But he knows that the nomination campaign is only the first step toward the presidency and that he must ask whether Kennedy has a better chance of winning the office than Carter. If he decides that Carter has a better chance of winning, he might decide to support the president, even though on a strict comparison of utilities, Kennedy merits support.

Consider two lotteries as ways of illustrating the decision problem the activist faces. In the first lottery, 10 people have equal chances at the prize, $100. In the second, 1000 people have equal chances at the prize that is now $500. Assume that a player's "utility" is simply the payoff from winning the lottery (rather than say, the joy of playing or taking risks). Because it is a lottery, we are comfortable thinking about odds or probabilities, and we are likely to ask not merely "How large is the payoff?" but "What are my chances of winning (something)?" Indeed, given a choice between playing in the first or the second lottery, a rational actor would enter the 10 person game with a smaller absolute payoff than in the 1000 person game. The reason is obvious: his expected utility is higher in the first than in the second game. He must discount the absolute payoff by the chances that he will receive it. Assuming all other things are equal, the expected utility associated with the first lottery is $10 ($10 = .10*$100), while the expected payoff from the second game is $.50 ($.50 = .001*$500). In other words, given a choice, the rational player will take the better chance at the smaller prize and forgo the lesser chance at the larger payoff.

We believe most people would choose the first over the second lottery because most people can make fairly simple rational calculations of the sort the choice requires.[1] Moreover, the problem facing the presidential activists in deciding whom to support for their party's nomination is analogous to the choice between the two lotteries, although the calculation of probabilities and payoffs no doubt is much more difficult. We assume the payoff from participating in the nomination process is directly linked to the activist's desire to select a candidate who will promote pleasing policy outcomes. But we have already argued that is not the only (or even the primary) motivating factor, just as "entering a lottery with the largest prize" is not the only motivating factor for someone who wishes to win prize money. The activist, too, is engaged in a kind of lottery and must decide whom to support based on the policy payoff discounted by the probability that the candidate will win the general election. The decision to support a particular candidate, therefore, will involve the calculus:

$$P_A^* U_A$$

where,

> P_A = the activist's subjective probability that candidate A will win the general election; and
>
> U_A = the policy utility the activist would receive from the candidate's election.

But activists are usually faced with a choice between (or among) contenders for the party's nomination. Therefore, a complete specification of the calculus of candidate choice must involve a comparison of contenders. To simplify things, and consistent with our analysis throughout this book, we focus upon activists choosing between the two major contenders in each party: Carter versus Kennedy among Democrats, and Reagan versus Bush among Republicans. The calculus of candidate choice, then, is a comparison of the expected utilities associated with each candidate:

$$P_A^* U_A - P_B^* U_B \tag{1}$$

where,

P_A and P_B are as before;

P_B = the probability the opposition candidate within the party will win; and

U_B = the policy utility the activist would receive from the opposition candidate's election.

When the expected utility associated with candidate A is greater than the expected utility linked to his opposition, candidate B, the activist will support candidate A. Where the expected utility of the opposition is greater, the model predicts the activist will support the opposition. Where the expected utilities are equal, the model is incapable of making a prediction.

An expected utility model of the sort depicted in equation (1) is not a new idea, although up until now, no study has systematically incorporated a model into an empirical study of activists' candidate choice. In explaining how citizens will choose candidates to support before the nominating conventions, John Aldrich (1980, p. 82) puts the matter succinctly: "The rational citizen is assumed to maximize expected utility. In a multicandidate contest, citizens must consider two factors; their preferences over the candidates and the chance each candidate has to win the . . . election." This understanding of activists' decision making is contrary to the purist model's view that activists seek only to maximize their ideological utility. As James Coleman puts it: "party electorates are not merely expressive voters, electing that candidate as their nominee whom they themselves find most appealing. Instead, they elect a candidate with some view toward the final election. If their interest is in maximizing their gains in the main election, they would certainly not be doing so if they nominated an extreme candidate who had no chance of election, no matter how fully he satisfied their tastes." Accordingly, Coleman (1972, p. 334) concludes that participants in the nomination campaign "will be voting to maximize an expected gain, and the expected gain is a product of two factors: the gain from this candidate if elected and the probability that this candidate will be elected." This is precisely what our equation (1) expresses in comparing the expected utilities associated with the major contenders within a party.[2]

In sum, we have two traditions in the literature on activists participating in the nomination campaign. One tradition, which we have cited widely throughout the book, is based upon surveys of participants and typically has relied upon respondents' own assessments of their approach to the possible tension between electability and ideology. This literature, probably the more

visible tradition in the field, concludes that contemporary
activists are purist, preferring to support candidates who are
ideologically compatible even if those candidates are not the
most electable. The second tradition has relied upon deductive
"rational choice" modeling and has not actually tested its theoretical expectations with data. Yet the prediction the rational
choice literature makes about activists' candidate support is
quite different from (and, we believe, more plausible than)
the purist model. We adopt the theoretical posture of the
rational choice literature coupled with the research methodology
of the survey. The question is, does the model portrayed in
equation (1) work when it is tested with the data?

A TEST OF THE INTRAPARTY EXPECTED
UTILITY MODEL

Equation (1) posits an intraparty comparison of leading
candidates and is the simplest plausible model of candidate
choice. We begin our analysis with the intraparty model that
ignores the opposition party, and then we move to a version
that considers the opposition party as well.

The operationalization of equation (1) is very straightforward and involves using already familiar measures. We
measure "utility" with our ideological proximity measures,
thereby equating the concept with general ideological satisfaction.
We have shown in various ways that our respondents are quite
ideological and that most of the issues debated during the 1980
campaign relate quite strongly to a general liberal-conservative
dimension. Thus, for now, we assume ideological proximity
captures policy utility, recognizing that this simplifying assumption does some (but not much) violence to the reality. Once
we have tested the model, we will be able to assess how much
we are giving up by ignoring specific issues.[3]

We did not ask respondents for precise probability estimates
of each candidate's chances in the general election, but we have
an excellent surrogate measure in our electability estimates.
The endpoints of the response dimensions on a five-point scale
nicely correspond with probabilities of 0 ("Definitely would lose")
and 1 ("Definitely would win"). We have scaled the remaining
responses proportionately to correspond with their "true" probability values.[4] In Figure 6.1 we present the theoretical relationship between candidate choice and the intraparty comparison of
expected utilities. The x axis represents the comparison of
expected utilities associated with candidate A and his major

FIGURE 6.1

Theoretical Relationship between Intraparty Expected Utility
Comparison and Candidate Preference

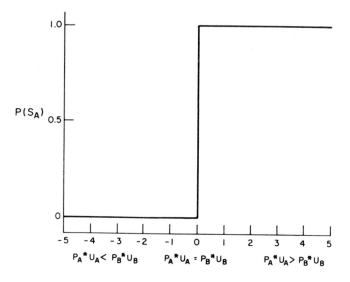

Where,

$P(S_A)$ = The Probability of Supporting Candidate A for the Party's
Nomination;

P_A = The Activist's Subjective Probability that Candidate A
will Win the General Election if Nominated by His Party;

U_A = The Ideological Utility the Activist would Receive from
Election of Candidate A as President;

P_B = The Activist's Subjective Probability that the Opposition
Candidate for the Party's Nomination will Win the
General Election if Nominated by His Party;

U_B = The Ideological Utility the Activist would Receive from the
Opposition Candidate's Election as President.

opposition for the party's nomination (candidate B). The ideological utility scores range from 1 (low ideological proximity)
through 5 (highest ideological proximity), and the probability
scores range from 0 through 1.0. The expected utilities, therefore, range from -5 through 5 and reflect the comparisons
between the candidates posited by the model. The dependent
variable is the probability of supporting the candidate (measured
by an expression of choice between the two candidates). So
long as the expected utility comparison even slightly favors
the opposition candidate, the score will be negative, and the
model predicts a zero probability of choosing the candidate.
When the expected utility comparison is equal, the model makes
no prediction (a .5 probability of choosing candidate A), and

when the comparison is positive, the model asserts a probability of 1.0 of supporting candidate A.

Figures 6.2 and 6.3 present the relationships between comparative expected utilities, and candidate support for the Democrats and Republicans respectively. Take the Democrats in Figure 6.2 as an example. The independent variable is the comparison of the expected utilities associated with Kennedy and Carter. A negative score indicates that the comparison favors Kennedy, while a positive score is pro-Carter. We have grouped the data according to the expected utility comparison and within each group calculated the percent supporting Carter. The graph summarizes the relationship, then, because each data point reflects the percentage supporting Carter for activists grouped on the expected utility dimension.[5] In Figure 6.3, the analysis is performed in an identical way except that the expected utility comparison involves Reagan and Bush, and the Y axis is defined as the percentage in each group choosing Reagan.

The data in both figures show a remarkably good fit to the expectations depicted in Figure 6.1. In both parties, activists scoring on the positive side of the expected utility comparison supported overwhelmingly the predicted candidate, either Carter or Reagan. Similarly, those predicted to support Kennedy or Bush do so by a very large margin, although there is more scatter among Republicans who "should" prefer Bush than among Democrats predicted to support Kennedy. Not surprisingly, there is more scatter near the zero points of each graph. Error in the model close to the zero point accounts for the "S" shape to the graph rather than the precise step-function predicted by Figure 6.1.

AN INTERPARTY EXTENSION OF THE MODEL

The intraparty model assumes that activists do not watch what the other party is doing (beyond considering the probability that the different contenders within their own party will win the general election) in deciding whom to support for the nomination. But it is possible that the disutility associated with the opposition party's candidate should be taken into account. Assume that a Democratic activist believes that Carter is certain to win the general election if nominated [$P_C = 1.0$] and that Kennedy "probably would win" the November election if nominated by his party [$P_K = .75$]. At the same time, however, assume that the activist perceives himself as perfectly proximate to

FIGURE 6.2

Relationship between Carter and Kennedy Expected Utility
Comparisons and Probability of Supporting Carter among
Democrats

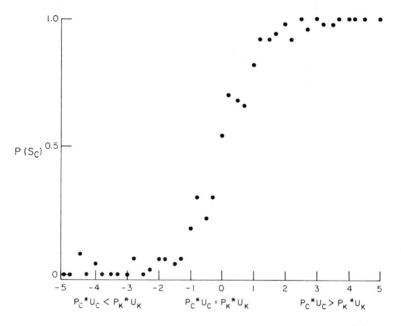

Where,

P(S_A) = The Probability of Supporting Carter for the Democratic
Nomination;

P_C = The Activist's Subjective Probability that Carter will Win the
General Election if Nominated by the Democrats;

U_C = The Ideological Utility the Activist would Receive from
Carter's Election as President;

P_K = The Activist's Subjective Probability that Kennedy will Win
the General Election if Nominated by the Democrats;

U_K = The Ideological Utility the Activist would Receive from
Kennedy's Election as President.

Kennedy [$U_K = 5$] while his proximity score to Carter is not as
strongly favorable [$U_C = 3$]. By the logic of our intraparty
model, the activist would compare the expected utilities associated
with Carter and Kennedy as follows:

$$[(1.0*3)-(.75*5)] = -.75$$

Because the activist's score is negative, the model predicts that
he will support Kennedy. In other words, the fact that Carter
is more electable than Kennedy is offset by the activist's substan-

FIGURE 6.3

Relationship between Reagan and Bush Expected Utility Comparisons and Probability of Supporting Reagan among Republicans

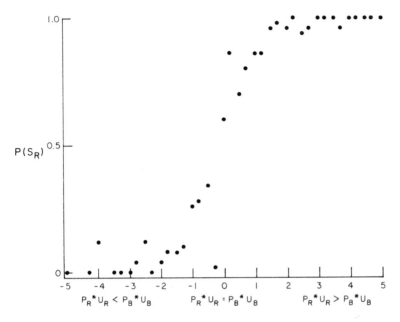

Where,

P(S_R) = The Probability of Supporting Reagan for the Republican Nomination;

P_R = The Activist's Subjective Probability that Reagan will Win the General Election if Nominated by the Republicans;

U_R = The Ideological Utility the Activist would Receive from Reagan's Election as President;

P_B = The Activist's Subjective Probability that Bush will Win the General Election if Nominated by the Republicans;

U_B = The Ideological Utility the Activist would Receive from Bush's Election as President.

tially greater utility from a Kennedy presidency over that offered by another Carter term. Note that while the model predicts that this activist will choose Kennedy, the score is only weakly in the Kennedy direction. How might an interparty model alter the prediction in this hypothetical case?

An interparty comparison involves the notion of disutility. An activist might base his or her choice in part upon a desire to avoid disaster—that is, the election of the opposition party's candidate. By including the probability of a candidate's election in our model we are already including a desire on the part of activists to avoid such disaster. Our interparty model merely adds an additional weight to the calculus that explicitly includes the disutility associated with the opposition party's front-runner:

$$(P_A{*}U_A - P_B{*}U_B) + [(5/U_F{*}P_F){*}(P_A - P_B)] \qquad (2)$$

where,

> $5/U_F$ = the disutility associated with the opposition party's front-runner[6] candidate for the nomination;
>
> P_F = the opposition party's probability the front-runner will win the election.

Equation (2) adds a weight associated with the expected disutility of the opposition party's candidate. Recall that the intraparty model predicts that our hypothetical Democratic activist will support the Kennedy challenge to Carter based upon a pro-Kennedy score of -.75. Assume, however, that the activist finds the GOP front-runner, Ronald Reagan, totally unacceptable on ideological grounds. According to our five-point scale, then, he would receive a utility score of 1 for Reagan. We take the reciprocal of this score and weight it by the activist's judgment of how electable Reagan would be if nominated (assume P_R = .75) in our example. This expected disutility term is itself weighted by the compared probabilities of the two Democratic contenders' election (in this example $[P_C - P_K]$ = 1.0 - .75 = .25). The full candidate support calculus using the inter-party model thus appears as follows:

$$[(1.03{*}3) - (.75{*}5)] + [(5/1){*}.75]{*} \ (1.0 - .75)$$

$$= \qquad -.75 \qquad + \qquad .938$$

$$= \qquad .188$$

As a result of adding the interparty term, our activist's weak preference for Kennedy is changed to a weak preference for Carter. That is, in order to avoid the disutility associated with the Reagan candidacy, the activist is hypothesized to "think again" by weighting the disutility associated with the opposition by the comparative electability of the contenders within his own party.

Despite the plausibility of entering a comparison with the opposition party into the model, the data do not support the addition by increasing the predictive power of the model. By way of summarizing the analysis thus far, we present in Table

6.1 comparisons of the predictive power of four models of candidate preference. The ideological model is clearly inferior to electability, a point already well established in Chapter 5. Using electability rather than ideology to predict candidate preference results in a 30 percent net increase in predictive accuracy for the Democrats and a 26 percent net increase for the Republicans. At the aggregate level, ideology substantially overpredicts support for the nomination loser in both parties because many predicted Kennedy and Bush supporters chose against their purely ideological inclinations to support a winner. Using electability alone to predict candidate choice results in overpredicting support for the winner at the aggregate level because an electability-only model cannot accommodate ideological preferences (a defect the expected utility model is intended to remedy).

The intraparty expected utility model represents yet another improvement over both of the univariate models. Among Democrats, the model correctly predicts an impressive 89 percent of the cases, while among Republicans it predicts 85 percent of respondents' actual preferences. For both Democrats and Republicans, the model actually makes more errors than a simple electability model, but it greatly reduces the percentage of cases for which no prediction is possible and, discounting for the erroneous predictions, results in a net gain over electability of 5 percent added predictive power for both parties. At the aggregate level, the intraparty expected utility model results in only a 2 percent overprediction for Carter, and a 1 percent overprediction for Reagan among Republicans.

The success of the intraparty model is a tough act to follow, and the table shows that the interparty model is not up to the task. At the individual level, the performance of the two models is very nearly identical (although there are slight differences lost because of rounding error). At the aggregate level, the interparty model results in 4 and 2 percent overpredictions for Democrats and Republicans respectively. An in-depth analysis comparing the two models reveals there is some shifting of predicted candidate choice in both parties as a result of introducing the interparty term (as our example above suggests). But the gains in accurate predictions made by using equation (2) instead of the intraparty version are more than offset by new errors introduced by the interparty formulation.[7]

Our analysis thus far suggests several important conclusions. First, the expected utility model is supported in the data analysis. Activists are best understood as utility maximizers in their candidate choice behavior. They do not merely choose

TABLE 6.1

Predictive Power of Several Models of Candidate Preference

	Individual Level Predictions				Aggregate Predictions		
	A % Correct	B % Incorrect	C % No Prediction	A - B	% Predicted Frontrunner	% Actual Frontrunner	% Difference
Ideology only							
Democrats	65	19	16	46	54	69	-15
Republicans	61	15	24	46	63	80	-17
Electability only							
Democrats	82	6	12	76	75	69	+6
Republicans	76	4	19	72	83	80	+3
Intraparty expected utility (Equation 1)							
Democrats	89	8	3	81	70	68	+2
Republicans	85	8	7	77	81	80	+1
Interparty expected utility (Equation 2)							
Democrats	89	8	2	81	70	66	+4
Republicans	85	8	7	77	81	80	+1

the most electable candidate, and they certainly do not merely select the candidate who best represents their ideological preferences. They understand that the presidential nomination process is a two-stage affair and that they must think about both stages as they exercise their choice in the first. "Thinking about both stages" means that they weigh both their ideological interest and their interest in nominating a winner in deciding whom to support. Second, they do not appear to be concerned about what the opposite party is doing (beyond their considera-tion of candidate electability). We showed in Chapter 5 that there is a significant partisan bias in activists' judgments about candidate electability and that bias may effectively insulate them from concern about minimizing disutility from the opposition. It may also serve to reduce their decision costs. After all, equa-tion (2) is more complicated than equation (1), and parsimony is a virtue not only for theorists but also for decision makers. At any rate, we find no evidence that activists introduce an explicitly cross-party comparison in their calculus. And third, while we are impressed with the performance of our expected utility formulation, we nonetheless leave a minority of cases "unexplained." Although the average presidential activist fits the utility-maximizing model in his or her candidate preference, there are enough activists for whom the model does not work to merit further exploration.

THE NONUTILITY-MAXIMIZER: AN EXAMINATION OF THE RESIDUALS

In this section we explore the success rate of the expected utility model for several broad categories of variables. Because the intraparty version is the most successful of the two expected utility models, we focus exclusively upon it. We are concerned with four categories of variables in order better to understand what we may have left out of the model and to gain insight on what sorts of activists are most likely to fit the expected utility formulation: variables in the model itself, issue opinions, experi-ence in the party organization, and purism-pragmatism.

With respect to the variables in the model, an examination of Figures 6.2 and 6.3 shows that the greatest proportion of erroneous predictions is found close to the zero point on the comparative expected utilities axis. Activists close to zero on this dimension are nearly indifferent between the candidates (at least with respect to expected utilities), and they are there-fore more likely to be influenced by other factors. Table 6.2

TABLE 6.2

Analysis of the Expected Utility Model's Performance among Activists for Whom a Prediction Was Made

Democrats
$(P_C*U_C - P_K*U_K)$

Model performance	0≥1	1≥2	2≥3	3≥4	>4	Row %
% Correct prediction	69.9	90.0	97.2	99.5	99.6	92.0
% Error because of:						
Ideology	11.2	1.8	.3	0	0	2.2
Electability	6.3	1.0	0	0	0	1.2
"Irrationality"	12.7	7.2	2.5	.5	.4	4.5
Total	100.1%	100%	100%	100%	100%	100%
Weighted n =	(959)	(1,557)	(1,482)	(1,210)	(1,029)	

Republicans
$(P_R*U_R - P_B*U_B)$

Model performance	0≥1	1≥2	2≥3	3≥4	>4	Row %
% Correct prediction	75.5	89.9	96.1	98.8	99.7	91.5
% Error because of:						
Ideology	8.6	.8	.7	0	.1	2.0
Electability	.7	.3	0	0	0	.2
"Irrationality"	15.3	9.1	3.1	1.2	.2	6.3
Total	100.1%	100.1%	99.9%	100%	100%	100%
Weighted n =	(1,137)	(1,716)	(1,346)	(917)	(984)	

summarizes the performance of the model by relating the success rate (and rate and source of error) to the absolute value of the expected utility comparisons for both Democrats and Republicans.[8] For both parties, there is a monotonic increase in the success rate of the model as activists' expected utility calculations depart from indifference. Likewise, as the expected utility comparisons yield a higher absolute value, there is a monotonic decrease in the proportion of activists who are, in the model's terms, "irrational" (that is, who choose the candidate perceived to be least electable and least proximate ideologically).

Looking at the row marginal percentages, there are only slight differences between the parties in the success rates of the model. Ignoring as the table does those who are indifferent between the candidates, there is a difference of only .5 percent in the predictive success of the model. An inaccurate prediction can result either from an activist choosing against both his ideological and his electability judgments, or it can result from the activist's weighting of the variables failing to match the weighting specified in the model (for example, an activist who "overemphasizes" ideology).

Table 6.2 illustrates that the successful prediction rate of the model was virtually identical for the two parties, excluding activists predicted to be indifferent between the two contenders in their party. But recall from Table 6.1 that the intraparty model fails to make a prediction for 7 percent of the Republicans but only for 3 percent of the Democrats. In other words, the comparative expected utility calculations result in more than twice as many scores of "0" among Republicans than among Democrats. There are two ways in which the model results in a score of perfect indifference: if the probability and utility estimates for both contenders are identical or if the expected utility estimate for the candidate equals the expected utility estimate for his opponent ($P_A*U_A = P_B*U_B$). In the first case, the model cannot make a prediction because the respondent thought both candidates were equally electable and equally attractive ideologically whereas, in the second case, the model yields no prediction because the respondent judged the candidates to have perfectly offsetting strengths and weaknesses.

Of the Republicans for whom no prediction was possible (n = 458), fully 96 percent were cases where activists perceived no difference between Reagan and Bush on both ideological utility and their probability of getting elected. And the great majority of these activists were indifferent between the GOP contenders because they saw both candidates as very desirable.

Theirs was a quandary resulting from deciding between highly attractive candidates. Of the many fewer Democrats with a net expected utility score of 0 (n = 183), 63 percent saw Kennedy and Carter as equal on both ideology and electability. Thus in contrast to the Republicans, Democrats were more likely to have been indifferent in the terms of the model because of what they saw as offsetting strengths of Carter and Kennedy.[9]

There is a less dramatic difference between the parties in accounting for the virtually equal proportions of erroneous predictions by the model. Of the 8 percent erroneous predictions in both parties, just over half of the Democratic activists (52 percent) choose against both ideology and electability, while fully 75 percent of the Republican errors result from activists choosing against both variables. This finding suggests that Republicans were more likely to be strongly influenced by other variables in making their choice, and an excellent candidate for the missing variables is opinions on specific issues.

By equating our concept of utility with ideological proximity, we may be overlooking the utility activists attach to particular issues. Table 6.3 presents an analysis of the performance of the model by opinion on selected issues. We have chosen the two issues in each party that show the greatest difference in predictive accuracy across categories of opinion. We also report the average percent accurately predicted for each of the five response categories for all 13 issue questions.

For the Democrats, the issues that are associated with the greatest variation in the accuracy of the model are national health insurance and affirmative action.[10] In both cases, activists strongly in favor of the liberal position on the issue were not predicted as well by the model, and there is a regular increase in predictive accuracy as activists become more conservative. Indeed, the mean levels of predictive accuracy for all issues show that while the deviation across opinion categories is on average not as great as for the two issues shown, the model appears to be systematically biased against liberals. Put another way, liberal Democrats in 1980 weighted their ideological preferences more strongly than conservative Democrats. Despite the apparent influence of issues like national health insurance causing Democratic liberals to defect from their expected utility inclinations, it will not do to overstate the effect of the issues. For example, among those strongly in favor of national health insurance (an opinion that places them in agreement with one of Senator Kennedy's major issues in 1980), only 58 percent of the inaccurately predicted activists chose Kennedy. In other words, 42 percent of the expected utility model's errors among

TABLE 6.3

Percent Accurately Predicted by Expected Utility Model by Preference on Selected Issues

	Strongly Favor Liberal Position	Favor	Undecided	Oppose	Strongly Oppose Liberal Position
Democrats					
National health insurance	85	87	92	96	97
Affirmative action	85	90	91	92	94
Thirteen-issue average	87	88	89	91	93
Republicans					
Equal Rights Amendment	75	81	78	82	91
Abortion	79	79	86	86	92
Thirteen-issue average	83	83	83	84	88

activists strongly favoring national health insurance were predicted by the model to support Senator Kennedy, but, nonetheless, they preferred Jimmy Carter! These activists chose not
only against the expected utility model but also against their
strongly held preferences on one of the more salient issues of
the Democratic nomination campaign. And, among those calculated to be indifferent on the expected utility comparison but
strongly favoring national health insurance, fully 60 percent
chose against their inclinations on that issue and supported
Carter.

Among Republicans, there does not appear to be as strong
a bias associated with general ideology although the two issues
selected show a greater deviation in predictive accuracy than
the Democratic issues. Both the Equal Rights Amendment and
the abortion question were highly emotional and, some would
say, special interests. The expected utility model is considerably
better at predicting the candidate choice of GOP activists who
strongly oppose the ERA and abortion, than it was for those
who strongly favor the ERA and the prochoice position.

And the evidence is stronger for the Republicans that the
ERA and abortion issues actually produced defections from the
model's expectations. The ERA issue, for example, divided
the GOP candidates with Bush favoring ratification, and Reagan
quite visibly opposing the amendment. Among the activists
strongly favoring the ERA who show up as errors in the model
$(n = 79)$, 76 percent chose against the model's prediction that
they would favor Ronald Reagan and that with their issue preferences they would support George Bush. Still, of the activists
predicted by the model to be indifferent between the contenders,
52 percent went against their strong preference for the ERA
and supported Reagan.

Our analysis of the issues shows that there were indeed
activists motivated by strong concern about an issue to go
against the utility-maximizing model. A slightly greater percentage of the errors in the Republican party appear to be linked
to issue preferences than among Democrats, but in neither
party was the proportion very high. We conclude, therefore,
that our calculations of expected utility based upon the equation
of utility with general ideological predispositions does very little
harm to the predictive power of the model. This analysis also
shows, as we have argued all along, that activists are ideological
and that concerns about special interests that might motivate
some to behave contrary to their general inclinations do not
appear to be as strong as some observers of nomination politics
have supposed. Our data consistently show very little intrusion

of "special interest" politics in the candidate choice behavior
of presidential activists.

Thus far our concern with analyzing the errors of the
model has been with understanding what the model may have
left out. Next we move away from concepts closely related to
those included in the model to determine whether we can come
to an understanding of which activists are more (or less) likely
to be utility maximizers in their candidate choice behavior.

A plausible hypothesis offered in the literature on party
activists is that the amount of experience in the party organization influences the way in which the activist reaches a decision
about which candidate to support (Kirkpatrick 1976; Polsby
and Wildavsky 1980). The assumption is that presidential activists with a demonstrated commitment to the parties have a
sustained interest in promoting candidates who will win, whereas
those more peripherally associated with the parties will be more
concerned with pursuing their ideological interests. The argument has special appeal in light of the history of the parties in
the period following the reforms of the late 1960s and early
1970s. One source of stress for the party organizations in the
postreform period may have been the reformed presidential
nominating process, which drew many "amateurs" into the process. These amateurs, by maximizing their ideological interests
to the exclusion of the party's interest in nominating a winner,
may have contributed to the decline of the parties.

Our argument throughout this book has been that the
thesis needs another look because we find compelling evidence
in 1980 that activists in general were motivated to select a
winner. But the inability of the "amateur" or "purist" thesis
to explain activists' candidate choice does not mean that it
cannot provide some purchase on our goal of understanding
for whom the expected utility model is least applicable. If so,
we might expect the candidate choice behavior of those without
substantial experience in the parties to be less successfully
predicted by the expected utility model. We might also expect
those with less demonstrated attachment to the party organization to base their choice for the nomination upon their ideological
interests. Moreover, errors among those activists strongly
linked to the party organization can be expected to result from
an overemphasis on electability.

The most striking finding in Table 6.4, which presents an
analysis of the performance of the expected utility model by
several measures of experience in the party organizations, is
that the model performs almost equally well for activists with
relatively little organizational experience as for those with

TABLE 6.4

Analysis of the Expected Utility Model's Performance by Party Organizational Experience

Model Performance	Party Offices Held			Elected Offices Held		Years Active in Party			
	None	1-3	4 or More	None	One or More	0-5	5-10	10-20	20+
Democrats									
% Correct prediction	89	89	93	89	93	88	88	91	92
% No prediction	3	3	1	3	2	3	4	2	3
% Error because of:									
Ideology	3	2	1	2	1	3	2	2	1
Electability	2	1	2	1	1	1	1	1	2
"Irrationality"	4	5	3	5	3	5	5	5	3
Total	101%	100%	100%	100%	100%	100%	100%	101%	101%
Weighted n =	(2,567)	(3,418)	(436)	(5,552)	(869)	(2,456)	(1,433)	(1,344)	(1,146)
Republicans									
% Correct prediction	86	85	85	85	86	85	86	85	85
% No prediction	6	8	8	7	8	6	8	6	8
% Error because of:									
Ideology	2	2	2	2	2	2	2	2	2
Electability	0	0	0	0	0	0	0	0	0
"Irrationality"	6	6	6	6	5	6	5	6	6
Total	100%	101%	101%	100%	101%	99%	101%	99%	99%
Weighted n =	(2,015)	(4,014)	(529)	(5,651)	(907)	(2,403)	(1,415)	(1,500)	(1,186)

considerably more experience. Among Republicans, there is
no significant pattern in the data. The model performs at
least as well for those with no party office-holding experience,
for those without elected office experience, and for those active
in the party less than five years as it does for activists scoring
higher on these measures. Nor is there any significant variation
in the sources of error. Regardless of organizational experience
among Republican activists, there is relentless evidence that
supporting a candidate for ideological reasons produces error
in about 2 percent of the cases.

Among Democratic activists, there is a very weak tendency
for the success of the model to be associated with our measures
of organizational experience. For example, the model enjoys
an 89 percent rate of successful prediction of candidate preference among activists with no office-holding experience in the
party, while among those having held four or more offices,
the success rate is 93 percent. An identical 4 percent increase
in the predictive power of the model is associated with the other
two measures of party experience. There is an even weaker
(though still visible) tendency for activists with less experience
to depart from the model's prediction because of the effects of
ideology. These effects among Democratic activists are of the
weakest possible magnitude and, therefore, cannot challenge
the applicability of the expected utility model of candidate
choice. The model works extremely well for Democratic activists
with little organizational experience: it works a little better
for Democrats with much organizational experience.

Finally, an obvious question is whether the expected utility
model performs any differently for activists with differing scores
on the purism-pragmatism index. We have shown in Chapter 3
that most say they are "purists," preferring to pursue their
ideological preferences and not compromise to win. Of course
our analysis of electability in Chapter 5 and the expected utility
model itself show that activists do compromise, balancing their
ideological preferences with their clear interest in nominating
a winner. But can we show that activists adopting the purist
perspective account for a disproportionate number of errors
by the model? The data in Table 6.5 show that this expectation
is disappointed. Among Democrats, there is almost no difference
between purists and pragmatists in the success rate of the model.
And among Republicans, the results actually show that the
expected utility model—demanding as it does compromise between
ideology and the chances of victory—has more predictive success
among purists than among pragmatists! Partly, this is due to
a monotonic increase in the percent "no prediction" across the

TABLE 6.5

Analysis of the Expected Utility Model's Performance by Purism-Pragmatism

Model Performance	Democrats			Republicans		
	Purists	Mixed	Pragmatists	Purists	Mixed	Pragmatists
% Correctly predicted	89	89	92	86	82	78
% No prediction	3	3	1	6	8	10
% Error because of:						
Ideology	2	2	2	2	2	2
Electability	1	2	1	0	0	0
"Irrationality"	4	5	4	5	7	9
Total	99%	101%	100%	99%	99%	99%
Weighted n =	(4,307)	(963)	(690)	(4,303)	(1,049)	(680)

three categories of purism, but there were more errors among pragmatists than among purists (11 and 7 percent error respectively). Furthermore, in both parties purists were no more likely than pragmatists to choose a candidate against the prediction of the model because of the attraction of ideology.

SUMMARY AND CONCLUSIONS

Our analysis of the model, and of the residuals, argues for the expected utility formulation as the best general explanation for what motivates activists to support a candidate for their party's presidential nomination. The model is both plausible and powerful in predicting candidate choice. It works well even for activists who purport to eschew compromise in favor of supporting a candidate whom they find ideologically attractive. Among Republicans, we could find no variation in the success of the model with organizational experience, although there were slight differences evident among Democrats. Those more experienced in the Democratic organization were more likely to conform to the expected utility model and were slightly less likely to defect from its predictions for purely ideological reasons. Republicans were found to be slightly more influenced by "special" interests that apparently caused them to choose against the model, and they were also more likely to be indifferent between the contenders for the GOP nomination than the Democrats were between Carter and Kennedy.

Despite the qualifications and minor differences between the parties we find in our data, we are convinced the model represents an important insight about presidential activists generally. They are rational actors. They do not seek single-mindedly to support candidates on ideological grounds, for to do so might amount to a strategic decision to help the opposite party. They are aware of the two stages in the process and of the need to compromise with other participants. If they are not purist ideologues, neither are activists interested solely in winning. They are concerned about public policy, and they are active in order to help promote their version of the public good. Winning, therefore, is not "for its own sake," nor is it everything. It is the way in which competing versions of the public good are selected to occupy positions of legitimate authority. Without their ideological commitment, presidential activists would appear to be simply seekers after the prestige or status that comes to those who associate with a winner. Were they so motivated, they would have no difficulty changing party, for example, if it were clear the opposition party offered the better promise of victory. But the activists we surveyed would have great difficulty changing party precisely because they see the party, and its presidential nominee, as an important instrument of public policy.

That activists are rational utility maximizers in their candidate choice behavior permits the observation that the party organizations may be well placed in the 1980s for a period of sustained resurgence. Activist participants recognize the possible tensions between the first and second stages of the presidential selection process, and in choosing a candidate to support, they weigh ideological satisfaction against the chances each candidate has to win in the second stage. If the process is generally dominated by participants who follow this rule (or it is reformed to encourage more participants who use an expected utility formulation), the parties in the years ahead may be better equipped to balance competing demands placed upon them in the U.S. political system. The activist core of each party tends to be markedly off-center in its ideological preferences. Many see this as desirable insofar as it promotes relatively clear programmatic choice for the electorate and, hence, popular control over national policy. But others have pointed out that if national candidates respond to the ideological center of their parties, they will be out of step with the general electorate, and, hence, they will carry their party organizations to nothing but defeat (Page 1978). 1980 is perhaps atypical in that the winning candidate was also ideologically congenial to many activists in his party. But the more enduring point is that activists, in choosing candidates according to the expected utility model, are balancing the competing demands for choice between ideologically distinct parties, on the one hand, and viable, competitive organizations on the other. Political parties controlled by activists who are not necessarily "professionals" in the sense that their livelihoods depend upon party success, but who nonetheless are balancing competing values in a rational way, have good reason to look to the future with renewed optimism.

NOTES

1. Note that we are not claiming that people who participate in lotteries (especially those with large numbers of participants) calculate their expected utilities or always act rationally. Rather, we contend only that most people would choose rationally

between the two games we describe. Ward Edwards (1968) provides a useful summary of experimental work in psychology testing applications of expected utility models. He concludes "detailed analysis . . . indicates that substantial deviations from rationality seldom occur unless they cost little; when a lot is at stake and the task isn't too complex for comprehension, men behave in such a way as to maximize expected utility" (1968, p. 41).

2. Coleman's analysis is based upon the spatial modeling literature (cf. Downs 1957) in which it is often assumed that the electability of a candidate is directly linked to the candidate's centrism. Thus Coleman argues that there is a direct tradeoff between electability and ideology: "Since the probability in general declines as the candidate's position is shifted away from the overall population mean toward the party voter's more extreme position, the party voters whose own preference is extreme is under a cross pressure: a candidate who is highly acceptable to the electorate as a whole is highly likely to be elected, but he will not be much preferable to the opposing party's candidate. Yet a candidate who fully represents his position is unlikely to be elected" (Coleman 1972, p. 334). Our analysis in Chapter 5 has already demonstrated that in the minds of activists, the link between centrism and electability is tenuous at best. The "extremist" Republicans in 1980 demonstrated that, in this respect at least, they could have their cake and eat it too.

3. It is possible to conceive of "utility" as including non-policy components linked to the personal qualities (such as honesty or experience) of the candidate. We ignore this possibility in this study largely because we lack sufficiently precise measures.

4. We score the remaining response categories as follows: "probably would win" .75; "might win" .50; and "probably would lose" .25.

5. The data in Figures 6.2 and 6.3 are grouped into 41 equal interval groups on the expected utility comparison (x axis). The average number of cases per group for the Democrats in Figure 6.2 is 157; for the Republicans in Figure 6.3 the average is 160. Each point on the graphs, then, is the percent supporting Carter or Reagan within the group.

6. Equation (2) is one of a number of interparty models we have tried with the data, and it provides the best fit. For example, we experimented with defining the opposition "front-runner" as the contender perceived by the activist to be most electable, rather than merely assuming it is Carter (for all

Republicans) or Reagan (for all Democrats). But substituting the most electable candidate (which is usually Carter or Reagan in any case) actually results in a slight increase in error.
$5/U_F$ is a measure of the disutility associated with the opposition party's front-runner because the ideological proximity score (U_F) ranges in value from 1 to 5. Therefore, a low proximity score (for example, 1) is converted to a high disutility score (for example, 5).

   7. Rounding error masks the trivially stronger performance of the intraparty model at the individual level. A number of possible interparty formulations were tried, and all versions failed to equal the intraparty model.

   8. Table 6.2 excludes all cases for which a prediction was not possible, that is, $P_A*U_A - P_B*U_B = 0$.

   9. Another indication that Republican activists were generally more positively disposed toward the contenders in their party than Democratic activists were toward theirs is the higher mean expected utility scores for Reagan and Bush than for Carter and Reagan:

Mean Candidate Expected Utility Scores

	Democrats		Republicans
Carter	2.915	Reagan	3.185
Kennedy	1.835	Bush	2.127

   10. The issues are not identical to those with the greatest independent effect in Table 5.9 because there we were assessing the independent effects of ideology and electability rather than working with the expected utility model.

7

CONCLUSIONS: PRESIDENTIAL ACTIVISTS AND PARTY RESURGENCE

PARTY REFORM AND DECLINE

There is an overwhelming consensus among scholars, journalists, and politicians that U.S. political parties have been declining in importance in recent years. This decline has occurred despite, and some argue partially because of, substantial efforts at reforming the parties' rules and procedures to make them more open and responsive to the wishes of their supporters in the electorate. The proportion of U.S. voters who identify with the Democratic or Republican parties declined from about 75 percent in 1964 to only about 60 percent in 1980; split-ticket voting also became much more prevalent in the 1970s as voters based their decisions more on the candidates and issues than on traditional party loyalties; voter turnout declined as many Americans came to view the parties as irrelevant to the political process (Crotty and Jacobson 1980; Wattenberg 1981).

The decline of the parties in the electorate was accompanied by a decline in the role played by party organizations in the electoral process. The direct primary, growing reliance on the electronic media for campaign communications, and the professionalization of campaign management have contributed to a shift from party-centered to candidate-centered political campaigns (Crotty and Jacobson 1980). Whereas party organizations themselves may not have declined in strength and effectiveness (Gibson et al. 1983), the parties no longer enjoy a monopoly in the conduct of political campaigns; candidate organizations and Political Action Committees (PACs) now play major roles in conducting and financing state and national campaigns.

Reforms of the presidential nominating process after 1968 were intended to increase the influence of rank-and-file party supporters in the selection of the presidential candidate. The McGovern-Fraser reforms and similar though less drastic changes adopted by the Republican Party made it much more difficult for party and elected officials to control caucuses and conventions that selected the delegates to the national conventions. In addition, many states adopted presidential primaries, and by 1976 about three-fourths of the delegates to the Democratic and Republican national conventions were chosen in primaries (Marshall 1981).

The proliferation of presidential primaries since 1968 has drastically altered the nature of the nominating campaign. Voters rather than party leaders now determine who is nominated for the presidency by the two major parties. As a result, the influence of state and local party organizations in the presidential nominating process has been greatly diminished. While the primary system may be more democratic than its predecessor, the absence of any effective role for state and local party organizations in the selection of a presidential nominee removes a major incentive for the involvement of activists in the local and state party organizations and in the presidential campaign.

Critics of the post-1968 reforms of the presidential nominating process have argued not only that the proliferation of primaries has weakened the party organizations but also that the reformed caucus-convention process has increased the influence of issue-oriented amateur activists at the expense of party professionals. According to these critics, the danger to the party organizations is that the members of this "new presidential elite" are more concerned about selecting a candidate who shares their ideological interests than about selecting a candidate with broad electoral appeal (Kirkpatrick 1976; Kirkpatrick 1978; Ladd 1978; Polsby and Wildavsky 1980; Polsby 1983).

The evidence that we have presented concerning the characteristics, attitudes, and behavior of presidential activists in 11 caucus-convention states in 1980 indicates that the danger posed to the parties by the "new presidential elite" has been overstated. Indeed, our findings suggest that these activists may be a valuable resource in the effort to revitalize local and state party organizations.

REPRESENTATION

One criticism of the presidential nominating reforms is that, despite efforts to promote broader participation in the delegate selection process by rank-and-file party supporters, the new presidential activists are even less representative of their parties' voters than were prereform activists. Even during the 1950s, long before the era of party reform, Democratic and Republican national convention delegates were quite atypical of the voters in terms of their social background characteristics and ideological views. Democratic delegates were a good deal more liberal than Democratic identifiers in the electorate while Republican delegates were much more conservative than their party's supporters; both groups of delegates were much higher in socioeconomic status and educational attainment than the voters (McClosky, Hoffman, and O'Hara 1960). However, according to critics of the modern nominating reforms, because these reforms have increased the influence of issue-oriented amateur activists at the expense of party regulars, the new breed of presidential activists tend to be more ideologically extreme and, therefore, less representative of the views of the electorate than were the activists of the prereform era. Moreover, despite affirmative action policies and quotas aimed at increasing representation of women and racial minority groups, the new breed of presidential activists continue to be recruited very disproportionately from the upper-middle class, college educated stratum of U.S. society (Kirkpatrick 1976).

Another potential danger of the nominating reforms is that issue-oriented amateur activists will view themselves as representatives of special interest constituencies outside the party and will be more concerned about advancing the issue positions of these constituencies than with building a winning electoral coalition for their party. Whereas interest groups such as business, labor, and agriculture have long participated in the nominating processes of the two major parties, some of the newer "single-issue" or ideological interest groups (such as anti-abortion groups or women's rights organizations) appear to be more dogmatic and less willing to compromise their positions for the sake of party unity than the more traditional economic interest groups.

The evidence from our survey of presidential activists in 11 states in 1980 is consistent with the findings of other studies concerning the social background characteristics of contemporary party activists: large majorities of Democratic and Republican activists were college educated with family incomes well above the national average. However, both parties have made considerable strides in increasing the representation of women in party affairs: one-half of the Democratic delegates and two-fifths of the Republican delegates in these 11 states were women.

In one important respect, the demographic characteristics of the delegates did reflect the social composition of the party coalitions in the electorate: blacks and Hispanics were much better represented among Democratic than among Republican presidential activists. About one-eighth of Democratic activists were members of a racial minority group (primarily blacks and Hispanics with smaller numbers of Asian-Americans and American Indians) compared with only 2 percent of Republican activists.

Despite the importance placed by both parties, and especially by the Democrats, in recent years on increasing the representation of specific demographic groups in party affairs, there was almost no relationship between these social background characteristics and the behavior of activists in choosing a presidential nominee. Women, members of racial minority groups, and young people in both parties displayed preferences among the contenders for the parties' nominations very similar to those of other delegates. There is no evidence in our data that activists viewed themselves as representatives of demographic groups when it came to selecting a presidential candidate. Thus, while the presence of blacks, Hispanics, women, and young people at the party conventions may be of considerable symbolic importance, especially to members of these groups, it had little influence on the decisions made by these conventions.

Majorities of Democratic and Republican delegates were active in at least one organized interest group in addition to their party activities. Labor unions, teacher organizations, women's rights groups, and civil rights organizations were much better represented at Democratic than at Republican conventions; business interests, religious organizations, and anti-abortion groups were better represented at Republican than at Democratic conventions. Moreover, these differences between the two parties were fairly consistent across all 11 states. In presidential politics, at least, the two major parties seem to represent the same interest groups in all states, regardless of region, interparty competition, or demographic composition.

Despite the high level of interest group activity among the delegates, interest group affiliation had very little influence on candidate preferences. With the exception of antiabortion activists in the Republican Party, who were almost unanimous in their support for Ronald Reagan, members of single-issue or ideological interest groups displayed candidate preferences similar to those of other delegates. There is little evidence that delegates acted as representatives of special interest groups in choosing a presidential candidate.

Differences between the types of interest groups represented by Democratic and Republican activists were reflected
by differences between the ideological orientations and issue
positions of activists in the two parties. Almost three-fifths
of Democratic delegates in our 11 states described themselves
as liberals while almost 90 percent of Republican delegates
described themselves as conservatives. On a wide variety of
domestic and international issues, Democratic activists were
consistently more liberal than Republican activists. Moreover,
whereas there was some variation in the ideologies of Democratic
and Republican delegates among the 11 states, Democratic
activists were substantially more liberal than Republican activists
in every state. The most liberal group of Republican delegates
were much more conservative than the most conservative group
of Democratic delegates. Despite differences in political traditions, economic conditions, and demographic patterns, Democratic and Republican presidential activists in all 11 states were
similar in their ideological orientations and issue positions.

Democratic activists were much more divided in their issue
preferences than Republican activists. Of the 13 national issues
included in our survey, only the question of a constitutional
amendment to prohibit abortion caused more division among
Republican than among Democratic activists. Nor was this
difference between the parties due simply to a regional split
between the northern and southern wings of the Democratic
Party: Republican activists were much more united in their
issue preferences than Democratic activists in all 11 states.
By 1980, a conservative ideological consensus appears to have
developed in the Republican Party. Whereas Barry Goldwater's
conservatism had divided the GOP in 1964, Ronald Reagan's
conservatism served to unify the party in 1980. In contrast,
Democratic activists were sharply split on a wide range of
issues. Despite Jimmy Carter's relatively easy nomination
victory over Edward Kennedy, the ideological divisions among
the ranks of Democratic activists may have complicated the task
of uniting the party in the general election campaign.

Given the ideological polarization of the two parties, the
danger of activists choosing "extremist" candidates and thereby
alienating large numbers of voters would appear to be real.
However, the severity of this danger depends upon the extent
to which activists base their choice of a candidate on ideological
grounds. Our analysis indicates that ideology and issue positions had a clear but limited influence on the choice of a presidential candidate by Democratic and Republican activists in
1980. Among Democratic activists, as expected, liberal self-

identification and issue positions were related to support Edward
Kennedy. However, even among the liberal activists who constituted Edward Kennedy's natural ideological constituency
within the Democratic Party, there were large-scale defections
to President Carter. Seventy-two percent of liberal Democratic
activists perceived Edward Kennedy as closer to their own
ideological position than Jimmy Carter. Nevertheless, these
activists preferred Carter over Kennedy for the Democratic
nomination by a margin of 50 to 36 percent. It was Senator
Kennedy's failure to attract greater support among his fellow
liberals that was largely responsible for his decisive defeat
among these Democratic activists.

Among Republican activists, too, ideology had only a
limited influence on candidate preference. George Bush made
his strongest showing, as expected, among the small minority
of moderate-to-liberal Republican activists. Even among this
group, however, Bush ran only even with Ronald Reagan.
The large majority of moderate-to-liberal Republicans, and a
plurality of moderate conservatives, viewed Bush as closer to
their own ideological position than Reagan. However, among
Republican activists who felt closer to Bush's ideology than
to Reagan's ideology, a plurality supported Ronald Reagan for
the Republican nomination. Like Edward Kennedy, George
Bush lost badly because he failed to win the support of many
activists in his party who shared his ideological orientation.
Like Jimmy Carter, Ronald Reagan won easily because he
gained the support of many activists in his party who disagreed
with his ideological orientation. The question this raised was:
Why did many activists in both parties ignore their ideology
and issue positions in choosing a presidential candidate?

POLITICAL STYLE

Our findings regarding the limited influence of ideology
on candidate choice appear to contradict the prevailing view
that contemporary party activists tend to be purists, more
concerned about advancing their issue positions than about
winning elections. Yet, when presented with a choice in the
abstract between ideological purity and electoral appeal, overwhelming majorities of Democratic and Republican activists
expressed a preference for ideological purity. Even among
delegates with experience in party or elected office, whom we
would expect to take a more pragmatic approach to politics,
purist attitudes predominated. The problem was that the purist

attitudes expressed by most Democratic and Republican activists had very little influence on their behavior in choosing a presidential candidate. Most activists do not appear to connect their support for ideological purity as a set of general principles with the practical task of choosing among several presidential contenders with differing ideological positions and claims to electability.

CANDIDATE CHOICE: IDEOLOGY
VERSUS ELECTABILITY

Choosing a candidate is the most important responsibility of presidential activists. We have argued that in order to understand this decision-making process, it is necessary to examine the tradeoff between ideology and electability in the context of the choice among a set of specific candidates and to directly measure activists' perceptions of those candidates' ideological positions and electoral prospects. When we move from the choice between ideology and electability in abstract to the choice between specific candidates with differing ideological positions and claims to electability, the choice that activists really face, we find that they behave rather pragmatically: in both parties, perceptions of electability had a much stronger influence on candidate choice than perceptions of ideological proximity. The most important reason why Jimmy Carter and Ronald Reagan were victorious in these 11 caucus-convention states is that the delegates attending the party conventions viewed them as more electable than their opponents.

That Jimmy Carter was viewed by most Democratic activists (and by most Republican activists) as more electable than Edward Kennedy is not surprising. Despite the economic and international problems that he faced, Jimmy Carter was the incumbent, and incumbency does have significant advantages in presidential elections. Denying renomination to Carter would have amounted to a renunciation of their party's record. There were serious questions about Edward Kennedy's character and competence. Finally, Jimmy Carter was clearly more of an ideological moderate than Edward Kennedy, and, according to the conventional wisdom of U.S. politics, a moderate should be more electable than a candidate with more extreme views.

It is more surprising that Ronald Reagan was overwhelmingly viewed by Republican activists (and by Democratic activists) as more electable than George Bush. Neither Reagan nor Bush had held elected national office, although Reagan's electoral record was certainly more impressive than Bush's—two terms as governor of California versus one term in the U.S. House of Representatives and an unsuccessful senate race in Texas. But George Bush was clearly more of a moderate than Ronald Reagan. Why wasn't Barry Goldwater's heir as the leader of the conservative wing of the GOP viewed as "another Goldwater?"

Not surprisingly, party activists tended to view the candidate they preferred on ideological grounds as the one most likely to win the November election. But perceptions of electability were not just rationalizations of activists' ideological preferences. About one-third of the delegates in each party perceived a conflict between their ideological preference and their perceptions regarding the electoral prospects of the candidates. Among the delegates perceiving such a conflict, more than three-fourths in each party supported the candidate whom they viewed as more electable.

One reason that Ronald Reagan was not viewed as "another Goldwater," despite his conservatism, is that neither Democratic nor Republican activists viewed ideological moderation as much of an electoral advantage. Perceptions of the relative centrism of Jimmy Carter and Edward Kennedy were only weakly related to perceptions of their relative electability, and perceptions of the relative centrism of Ronald Reagan and George Bush were completely unrelated to perceptions of their relative electability.

Our findings suggest that activists view a candidate's electoral record, personality, and ability to wage an effective campaign as more important factors in assessing electability than ideology or issue positions. It is also possible, given the dynamic nature of the prenomination campaign, that perceptions of electability are influenced by the outcomes of earlier primaries and caucuses (Aldrich 1980). A candidate who does well may be perceived, correctly or incorrectly, as more electable than a candidate who does poorly.

How activists evaluate candidates' electoral prospects is a crucial question that should be addressed in future research. The factors that influence activists' evaluations may vary over time, depending upon the political climate in the country. Thus, in 1980, the widespread perception that a conservative mood was sweeping the country, whether accurate or inaccurate, may have caused activists in both parties to take a more favorable view of Ronald Reagan's electoral prospects: activists may have perceived liberalism as an electoral liability among Democratic candidates even though they did not view conservatism as a liability among Republican candidates. Activists' evaluations of candidates' electoral prospects may not always be realistic; at the 1972 Democratic national convention, for example, most of the McGovern delegates thought that George McGovern had the best chance of winning the presidential election of any candidate in either party (Stone and Abramowitz 1983). However, our findings do indicate that activists are concerned about electability as well as ideology. Activists may also learn from their failures; having seen their party's candidate suffer a crushing defeat in the 1972 presidential election, many liberal Democratic activists may have been wary about nominating "another McGovern" in 1980.

PRESIDENTIAL ACTIVISTS AS RATIONAL ACTORS

The presidential campaign does not end with the nominating convention. Regardless of how well a candidate represents the ideological views of party activists, that candidate cannot implement any policies without winning the general election. The evidence that we have presented shows that party activists recognize these facts and behave accordingly. We have proposed and tested an expected utility model of candidate choice. According to this model, activists discount the ideological "payoffs" expected from candidates by their chances of winning the general election.[1] This model was more successful at predicting the candidate preferences of Democratic and Republican activists in 1980 than a model based on electability alone; it was far more accurate than a model based on ideology alone. The expected utility model worked very well for both "purists" and "pragmatists" and for both experienced and inexperienced activists. Regardless of their political style or previous involvement in party affairs, presidential activists appear to behave rationally, given the constraints of the two-stage presidential selection process.

The finding that presidential activists weigh both ideology and electability in choosing a nominee has important implications for the type of choice that the parties present to the general electorate in November. Critics of the modern presidential nominating reforms (Kirkpatrick 1978; Ranney 1975; Polsby 1983) have argued that activists concerned solely with advancing their issue preferences will choose "extremist" candidates, thereby alienating large numbers of voters in the general election. However, there is also a danger that activists concerned solely with winning, lacking any issue or ideological commitments, will

choose candidates whose issue positions are so ambiguous or
so similar that the electorate will have no opportunity to choose
between contrasting policy alternatives. As Downs observed,
pure vote-maximizing behavior by political parties makes it
difficult for citizens to vote on a rational basis (1957, p. 136).

In reality, it is very unlikely that presidential activists
have ever been either pure issue maximizers or pure vote maximizers. Even the "pragmatic" party regulars who once controlled
presidential nominations had issue preferences. Many Democratic
party regulars refused to support George McGovern's candidacy
in the 1972 general election because of genuine opposition to
some of McGovern's issue positions as well as a belief that
McGovern was going to lose badly (Nakamura 1980). Even at
the 1972 Democratic national convention, which nominated George
McGovern, perceptions of the candidates' electoral prospects
had a very strong impact on delegates' candidate preferences
(Stone and Abramowitz 1983).

If activists weigh both ideology and electability in choosing
a nominee, it is very unlikely that the parties will nominate
candidates whose issue positions are indistinguishable. In the
first place, a candidate whose issue positions are very different
from those of most party activists will not receive a very high
expected utility rating no matter how electable he or she may
be. Very few liberal Democratic activists would support a
candidate like George Wallace, even if they thought he could
win in November. Very few conservative Republican activists
would support a candidate like John Anderson, even if they
believed that he had the best chance of any Republican candidate to defeat the Democratic nominee. Moreover, we have
seen that perceptions of candidates' electoral prospects are
influenced by activists' own ideological positions. They tend
to see the candidate they prefer on ideological grounds as the
most electable candidate. Although perceptions of candidates'
electability are far from being mere rationalizations of ideological
preferences, they are biased by these preferences. This bias
acts to reinforce the ideological preferences of party activists.

Despite the ideological bias in perceptions of candidates'
electoral prospects, activists cannot ignore such factors as
electoral performance, political experience, and character in
evaluating electability. If a candidate takes issue positions
that are clearly unpopular with a majority of the electorate, his
electoral prospects may also be downgraded. Thus, in 1980
many liberal Democratic activists came to the conclusion that
Edward Kennedy was either too liberal or too tarnished by
personal problems to make an effective presidential candidate.

Similarly many moderate Republicans decided that, despite his
relatively moderate ideological stance, George Bush did not
have either the political experience or the campaign ability
needed by a strong presidential candidate.

Because they want to win, party activists are unlikely to
go on an ideological binge, disregarding the electoral consequences of their decisions. If they misread the electorate's
preferences, as the Democrats did in 1972 and the Republicans
did in 1964, they will probably learn from their mistakes. The
specter of "another McGovern" has haunted Democratic party
activists since 1972 just as the specter of "another Goldwater"
haunted Republican activists in the aftermath of 1964. Conservative "extremist" Barry Goldwater was succeeded by the
more moderate Richard Nixon as the GOP nominee in 1968.
Liberal "extremist" George McGovern was succeeded by the
more moderate Jimmy Carter in 1976. However, concern with
electability need not result in the nomination of "me too" candidates by the parties. Winning is a means to an end and not
simply an end in itself. Activists want to win in order to obtain
their policy objectives. Moreover, the results of the 1980
presidential election suggest that moderation in the pursuit
of victory is not necessarily a virtue. Giving the voters
"a choice and not an echo" can be a pragmatic strategy.

PRESIDENTIAL ACTIVISTS AND
PARTY RESURGENCE

The proliferation of presidential primaries since 1968 has
relegated state and local party organizations to a minor role in
the nomination of the presidential candidates. The national
party conventions, which were once an opportunity for bargain-
ing and coalition building among state and local party leaders,
now merely ratify the decisions made by the voters in presidential primaries. Instead of courting party leaders and activists,
presidential candidates wage expensive advertising campaigns
in the mass media to appeal to potential primary voters. As a
result, the successful presidential candidate, once elected,
may feel little obligation to the party organization. For their
part, the party's leaders, including its elected officials, may
feel little obligation to the president. The experience of the
Carter presidency provides an illustration of these dangers:
in his cabinet appointments, in his relationships with Congress,
and in his attempts to cope with his political misfortunes, Jimmy
Carter showed little recognition of any responsibility to his

party's leaders or to the constituencies that comprise the Democratic electoral coalition (Polsby 1983, pp. 89-130).

The proliferation of presidential primaries has also removed an important incentive for participation in state and local party organizations: the opportunity to influence the presidential nomination. Without patronage to reward those who contribute their time and effort, most party organizations must rely on intangible rewards. But without any influence over the selection of candidates, the party organization provides little opportunity for activists to fulfill their purposive goals.

One of the major reasons that many state parties adopted presidential primaries in place of caucus-convention proceedings after 1968 was a fear that reformed party caucuses and conventions would be captured by issue-oriented candidate enthusiasts with little concern for the party organization (Polsby 1983, p. 62). However, our examination of the characteristics, attitudes, and behavior of delegates attending reformed party conventions in 11 states in 1980 leads us to the conclusion that these presidential activists pose less of a threat to the viability of state and local party organizations than does the steady increase in the number of states holding presidential primaries.

Because voters in presidential primaries have much less commitment to the party as an organization than party activists, it seems unlikely that they give as much consideration to the candidates' electoral prospects. Although turnout in primary elections is generally much higher than turnout for party caucuses, primary voters may give greater weight to ideological concerns in selecting a nominee than activists attending party caucuses. As a result, presidential primaries may produce a weaker candidate than a caucus-convention system dominated by party activists (Lengle 1981).

The large majority of presidential activists in these 11 caucus-convention states were strong partisans and dedicated party workers. Many compromised their personal ideological preferences in selecting a presidential candidate who appeared to offer the best chance of winning in November. In contemplating further nominating reforms, the parties could do far worse than encouraging more states to consider the caucus-convention system as an alternative to the presidential primary.

NOTES

1. One limitation of our model is that it assumes that the payoff that activists expect to receive is determined entirely

by a candidate's ideological proximity. This assumption is somewhat unrealistic, and future research on the candidate choice behavior of party activists should incorporate non-ideological as well as ideological payoffs. These may include personal qualities such as integrity and competence as well as stands on specific issues of particular importance to the activist. The potential importance of nonideological payoffs is suggested by our finding that perceived electability was a much better predictor of candidate choice than ideological proximity.

APPENDIX A
THE 1980 DELEGATE SURVEY

1. How long have you lived in (name of state)?
   1. Less than 5 years ( )
   2. Between 5 and 10 years ( )
   3. Between 10 and 20 years ( )
   4. More than 20 years ( )
2. How long have you been active in party politics in (name of state)?
   1. Less than 5 years ( )
   2. Between 5 and 10 years ( )
   3. Between 10 and 20 years ( )
   4. More than 20 years ( )
3. How would you describe the area where you now live?
   1. City with over 250,000 population ( )
   2. Suburb of city with over 250,000 population ( )
   3. City with between 100,000 and 250,000 population ( )
   4. Suburb of city with between 100,000 and 250,000 population ( )
   5. City with between 50,000 and 100,000 population ( )
   6. City with between 10,000 and 50,000 population ( )
   7. Town with less than 10,000 population ( )
   8. Rural area ( )
   9. Other ( )
4. What county is that in?
5. What congressional district do you live in?
6. Please indicate which, if any, of the following positions you now hold or have held in the past. (Check as many as apply.)

	Hold Now	Held in Past
Member of a local (city, county, or town) party committee......................	( )	( )
Chairman of a local party committee......	( )	( )
Other local party office.................	( )	( )
Member of congressional district party committee...........................	( )	( )
Member of state central committee........	( )	( )
Elected to state or national office........	( )	( )
Elected local office.....................	( )	( )

Appointed government or political office .. ( )   ( )
Paid campaign staff for candidate......... ( )   ( )

7. Before this convention, had you ever been a delegate to a state or national party convention?
   1. Yes ( )   2. No ( )

8. How often have you been actively involved in recent state and national political campaigns?
   1. Active in all ( )   3. Active in a few ( )
   2. Active in most ( )   4. Active in none ( )

9. What kinds of campaigns have you been active in? (Check as many as apply.)
   Local ( )   State Legislative ( )   Congressional ( )
   Stateswide offices ( )   Presidential ( )   Other ( )

10. Which of the following activities, if any, have you performed in political campaigns? (Check as many as apply.)
    Clerical work ( )   Writing ads, press releases ( )
    Door-to-door canvassing ( )   Speechwriting ( )
    Telephone canvassing ( )   Planning strategy ( )

11. How would you describe your own party affiliation:

    In state politics?
    1. Strong Democrat ( )
    2. Democrat, but not too strong ( )
    3. Independent, closer to Democrats ( )
    4. Completely independent ( )
    5. Independent, closer to Republicans ( )
    6. Republican, but not too strong ( )
    7. Strong Republican ( )

    In national politics?
    1. Strong Democrat ( )
    2. Democrat, but not too strong ( )
    3. Independent, closer to Democrats ( )
    4. Completely independent ( )
    5. Independent, closer to Republicans ( )
    6. Republican, but not too strong ( )
    7. Strong Republican ( )

12. DEMOCRATIC DELEGATES: Was there ever a time when you considered yourself a Republican?
    1. Yes ( )   2. No
    REPUBLICAN DELEGATES: Was there ever a time when you considered yourself a Democrat?
    1. Yes ( )   2. No ( )

13. IF YOU HAVE EVER CHANGED YOUR PARTY AFFILIATION:
    In what year did you last change your party affiliation?
    Year _____

14. Please indicate your opinion about each of the following statements. There are no right or wrong answers, so just give your personal opinion.

	1 Strongly Agree	2 Mildly Agree	3 Not Sure	4 Mildly Dis- agree	5 Strongly Disagree
A political party should be more concerned with issues than with winning elections	( )	( )	( )	( )	( )
The party platform should avoid issues that are very controversial or un-popular	( )	( )	( )	( )	( )
I'd rather lose an election than compromise my basic philosophy	( )	( )	( )	( )	( )
A candidate should express his convictions even if it means losing the election	( )	( )	( )	( )	( )
Broad electoral appeal is more important than a consistent ideology	( )	( )	( )	( )	( )

15. We're interested in your reasons for becoming actively involved in this year's presidential campaign. Please indicate how important each of the following factors was for you.

	1 Very Impor- tant	2 Some- what Impor- tant	3 Not Very Impor- tant	4 Not at All Impor- tant
To support my party	( )	( )	( )	( )
To help my own political career	( )	( )	( )	( )
To enjoy the excitement of the campaign	( )	( )	( )	( )
To meet other people with similar interests.........	( )	( )	( )	( )

To support a particular candidate I believe in	( )	( )	( )	( )
To work for issues I feel very strongly about......	( )	( )	( )	( )
To enjoy the visibility of being a delegate	( )	( )	( )	( )
To fulfill my civic responsibilities..................	( )	( )	( )	( )

16. How would you describe your own political philosophy?
    1. Very liberal ( )   4. Somewhat conservative ( )
    2. Somewhat liberal ( )   5. Very conservative ( )
    3. Middle-of-the-road ( )

17. Please indicate your opinion about each of the following state and national political figures.

	1 Very Favor-able	2 Some-what Favor-able	3 Neutral	4 Some-what Unfavor-able	5 Very Unfavor-able
Jimmy Carter.....	( )	( )	( )	( )	( )
Edward Kennedy..	( )	( )	( )	( )	( )
Jerry Brown......	( )	( )	( )	( )	( )
Ronald Reagan....	( )	( )	( )	( )	( )
George Bush......	( )	( )	( )	( )	( )
John Anderson....	( )	( )	( )	( )	( )
John Dalton	( )	( )	( )	( )	( )
Harry Byrd, Jr...	( )	( )	( )	( )	( )
John Warner......	( )	( )	( )	( )	( )
Charles Robb.....	( )	( )	( )	( )	( )
Marshall Coleman..	( )	( )	( )	( )	( )

18. Was there any particular issue that caused you to become involved in this year's election campaign?
    1. Yes ( )   2. No ( )
    IF YES: What issue was that? _____

19. Please indicate your position on each of the following issues.

	1 Strong-ly Favor	2 Favor	3 Unde-cided	4 Op-pose	5 Strong-ly Oppose
The Equal Rights Amendment to the U.S. Constitution	( )	( )	( )	( )	( )

A constitutional amend-
ment to prohibit abor-
tions except when the
mother's life is en-
dangered .... ( )   ( )   ( )   ( )   ( )
A substantial increase in
defense spending even
if it requires cutting
domestic programs ...... ( )   ( )   ( )   ( )   ( )
A government sponsored
national health insurance
program .... ( )   ( )   ( )   ( )   ( )
More rapid development
of nuclear power .... ( )   ( )   ( )   ( )   ( )
Across-the-board cuts in
nondefense spending to
balance the federal
budget.................. ( )   ( )   ( )   ( )   ( )
Affirmative action pro-
grams to increase
minority representation
in jobs and higher
education .... ( )   ( )   ( )   ( )   ( )
Deregulation of oil and
gas prices .... ( )   ( )   ( )   ( )   ( )
Mandatory wage-price
controls to deal with
inflation .... ( )   ( )   ( )   ( )   ( )
Stronger action to reduce
inflation even if it in-
creases unemployment
substantially .... ( )   ( )   ( )   ( )   ( )
Reinstituting draft
registration .... ( )   ( )   ( )   ( )   ( )
Ratification of the SALT II
Treaty................. ( )   ( )   ( )   ( )   ( )
Increasing U.S. military
presence in the Middle
East .... ( )   ( )   ( )   ( )   ( )

20. How would you rate the political philosophy of each of the
following presidential candidates?

	1	2	3	4	5
	Very Liberal	Some- what Liberal	Middle- of-the- Road	Some- what Conserv- ative	Very Conserv- ative
Jimmy Carter.....	( )	( )	( )	( )	( )
Edward Kennedy..	( )	( )	(,)	( )	( )
Jerry Brown......	( )	( )	( )	( )	( )
Ronald Reagan....	( )	( )	( )	( )	( )
George Bush......	( )	( )	( )	( )	( )
John Anderson....	( )	( )	( )	( )	( )

21. Please rank your preferences for your party's presidential nomination.

     1st choice: _____

     2nd choice: _____

     3rd choice: _____

22. Are you pledged to support a particular candidate at the convention?

     1. Yes ( )   2. No ( )

     IF YES: Which candidate is that? _____

23. How good a chance do you think each of the following candidates would have of winning the November election if nominated by his party?

	1	2	3	4	5
	Definitely Would Win	Probably Would Win	Might Win	Probably Would Lose	Definitely Would Lose
Jimmy Carter	( )	( )	( )	( )	( )
Edward Kennedy..	( )	( )	( )	( )	( )
Jerry Brown......	( )	( )	( )	( )	( )
Ronald Reagan....	( )	( )	( )	( )	( )
George Bush......	( )	( )	( )	( )	( )
John Anderson....	( )	( )	( )	( )	( )

24. Which, if any, of your party's candidates would you be unable to support in the November election? (Check as many as apply.)

     DEMOCRATS: Carter ( )   Kennedy ( )   Brown ( )

         I could support any of these ( )

     REPUBLICANS: Reagan ( )   Bush ( )   Anderson ( )

         I could support any of these ( )

25. How did you vote in the 1976 presidential election?

     1. Carter ( )   2. Ford ( )   3. Neither, didn't vote ( )

26. How would you rate the effectiveness of the Democratic and Republican state party organizations in (name of state)?

	1 Very Effective	2 Fairly Effective	3 Not Very Effective	4 Not at All Effective	8 Not Sure
Democratic organization..	( )	( )	( )	( )	( )
Republican organization..	( )	( )	( )	( )	( )

27. At present, how important a role does your state party organization play in each of the following areas?

	1 Very Important	2 Somewhat Important	3 Not Very Important	4 Not at All Important	8 Not Sure
Providing campaign assistance to candidates	( )	( )	( )	( )	( )
Taking positions on issues to influence elected officials	( )	( )	( )	( )	( )
Providing services and information to elected officials and local party organizations between campaigns	( )	( )	( )	( )	( )
Recruiting candidates.....	( )	( )	( )	( )	( )
Informing the electorate about party goals and positions	( )	( )	( )	( )	( )

28. How important a role do you think your state party organization should play in each of the following areas?

	1 Very Important	2 Somewhat Important	3 Not Very Important	4 Not at All Important	8 Not Sure
Providing campaign assistance to candidates	( )	( )	( )	( )	( )
Taking positions on issues to influence elected officials................	( )	( )	( )	( )	( )

Providing services and
information to elected
officials and local party
organizations between
campaigns .... ( )   ( )   ( )   ( )   ( )
Recruiting candidates..... ( )   ( )   ( )   ( )   ( )
Informing the electorate
about party goals and
positions................ ( )   ( )   ( )   ( )   ( )

29. In which of the following groups, if any, have you been
    politically active? (Check as many as apply.)
    Labor unions ( )
    Educational or teachers organizations ( )
    Other professional organizations ( )
    Business organizations ( )
    Church-related groups ( )
    Women's rights groups ( )
    Civil rights groups ( )
    Conservation or ecology groups ( )
    Public interest groups ( )
    Antiabortion groups ( )
    Farm or agricultural organizations ( )
    Other issue-related groups ( )

30. How politically active were your parents when you were
    growing up?

                          Father   Mother

    1. Very active .... ( )   ( )
    2. Fairly active .... ( )   ( )
    3. Not very active..... ( )   ( )
    4. Not at all active..... ( )   ( )
    5. Not sure .... ( )   ( )

31. In what state did you spend most of your childhood?

    _____

32. How would you describe your parents' party affiliation at
    the time when you were growing up?

                                            Father   Mother

    1. Strong Democrat ....   ( )   ( )
    2. Democrat, but not too strong........   ( )   ( )
    3. Independent, closer to Democrats....   ( )   ( )
    4. Completely independent ....   ( )   ( )
    5. Independent, closer to Republicans..   ( )   ( )
    6. Republican, but not too strong......   ( )   ( )

7. Strong Republican   ( )   ( )

8. Not sure   ( )   ( )

33. What is your approximate age?

    1. 18-24 ( )   5. 40-44 ( )   9. 60-64 ( )

    2. 25-29 ( )   6. 45-49 ( )   10. 65-69 ( )

    3. 30-34 ( )   7. 50-54 ( )   11. 70 or over ( )

    4. 35-39 ( )   8. 55-59 ( )

34. What is your sex? 1. Female ( )   2. Male ( )

35. What is your race?

    1. White ( )   3. Hispanic ( )   5. American Indian ( )

    2. Black ( )   4. Oriental ( )

36. What is your religious preference? (For example, Baptist, Methodist, Roman Catholic.)

    Religious preference _____

36a. Do you consider yourself to be either a fundamentalist or born-again Christian?

    1. Yes ( )   2. No ( )

37. In general, how religious do you consider yourself?

    1. Very religious ( )   3. Not very religious ( )

    2. Fairly religious ( )   4. Not at all religious ( )

38. How much formal schooling have you completed?

    1. None ( )

    2. Grade school only ( )

    3. Some high school ( )

    4. Graduated high school ( )

    5. Some college ( )

    6. Graduated college ( )

    7. Post college ( )

39. What would you estimate your family's income will be this year before taxes?

    1. 0-$14,999 ( )   4. $35,000-44,999 ( )

    2. $15,000-24,999 ( )   5. $45,000-59,999 ( )

    3. $25,000-34,000 ( )   6. $60,000 or more ( )

APPENDIX B
DATA COLLECTION AND
WEIGHTING PROCEDURES

The data analyzed in this study come from a survey of delegates attending party conventions in 11 states between April and June of 1980. These 11 states all utilized a caucus-convention process (rather than a primary election) to select their delegates to the 1980 Democratic and Republican presidential nominating conventions. Delegates attending the state conventions were responsible for electing the delegates to the national nominating conventions. In each state, a team of political scientists distributed and collected self-administered questionnaires. When possible, the questionnaires were attached to delegates' seats or included in packets of information distributed by the parties to delegates. Depending on the number of delegates at each convention, the questionnaires were distributed to all delegates or to a random sample of delegates. Clearly marked collection boxes were placed at exits and other locations around the convention sites to permit delegates to return completed questionnaires. In addition, whenever possible, members of the research teams circulated in the convention hall to collect questionnaires. The questionnaires used in each state were identical except for their covers, an introductory letter from the local research team, and a few optional questions dealing with state issues and political leaders.

The number of delegates attending state party conventions ranged from a few hundred to several thousand. In addition, because of variation in access to the convention floor and cooperation from party officials, the response rate also varied considerably.

Because the procedures used to distribute the questionnaires did not allow us to determine how many delegates actually received questionnaires, it is not possible to calculate a precise response rate for each state. However, the proportion of distributed questionnaires that were returned varied from approximately 25 to 70 percent, with an average of approximately 50 percent.

The following table shows the number of completed questionnaires returned at each party convention:

	DEMOCRATS	REPUBLICANS
Arizona	337	387
Colorado	1,003	638
Iowa	1,673	1,107
Maine	1,046	441
Missouri	317	380
North Dakota	623	403
Oklahoma	609	1,244
South Carolina	621	739
Texas	440	564
Utah	452	1,218
Virginia	1,669	1,716

A total of 17,628 delegates—8,790 Democratic delegates and 8,838 Republican delegates—returned completed questionnaires. We were able to compare the delegates who returned questionnaires with the entire population of delegates at each convention in terms of geographical distribution (by county or congressional district) and presidential candidate support. There was only one significant discrepancy: among Maine Democrats, delegates from one of the state's two congressional districts were over-represented among survey respondents. Although respondents from the two districts did not differ in presidential candidate support, we weighted the Maine Democratic delegates to equalize representation of the two districts.

Because of the large variation in the number of respondents at each state party convention, we weighted respondents to equalize the weight of each state party convention. All the overall results presented in this book are based on this weighted file and represent an average of the 11 states for each party. All state-by-state results are based on the unweighted data.

BIBLIOGRAPHY

In addition to the works cited in the text, we include a number of others that we have found instructive in thinking about the politics of presidential nominations.

Abramowitz, Alan I., John J. McGlennon, and Ronald B. Rapoport. 1981. Party Activists in Virginia. Charlottesville, Virginia: Institute of Government.

_____. 1983. "The Party Isn't Over: Incentives for Activism in the 1980 Presidential Campaign." Journal of Politics 45: 1006-15.

Abramson, Paul R., John H. Aldrich, and David W. Rhode. 1982. Change and Continuity in the 1980 Elections. Washington, D.C.: Congressional Quarterly Press.

Aldrich, John H. 1980. Before the Convention: Strategies and Choices in Presidential Nomination Campaigns. Chicago: University of Chicago Press.

_____, and Charles Cnudde. 1975. "Probing The Bounds of Conventional Wisdom: A Comparison of Regression, Probit, and Discriminant Analysis." American Journal of Political Science 19:571-608.

Aronson, Peter H., and Peter C. Ordeshook. 1972. "Spatial Strategies for Sequential Elections." In Models of Collective Decision Making, edited by Richard A. Niemi and Herbert F. Wiesberg, pp. 298-331. Columbus, Ohio: Merrill.

Axelrod, Robert. 1974. "Communication." American Political Science Review 68:717-20.

_____. 1972. "Where the Votes Come From: An Analysis of Electoral Coalitions, 1952-1968." American Political Science Review 66:11-20.

Brams, Steven J. 1978. The Presidential Election Game. New Haven: Yale University Press.

Campbell, Angus, Phillip E. Converse, Warren E. Miller, and Donald E. Stokes. 1960. The American Voter. New York: John Wiley & Sons.

Ceaser, James W. 1979. Presidential Selection: Theory and Development. Princeton: Princeton University Press.

_____. 1982. Reforming the Reforms: A Critical Analysis of the Presidential Selection Process. Cambridge, Massachusetts: Ballinger.

Coleman, James S. 1972. "The Positions of Political Parties in Elections." In Probability Models of Collective Decision Making, edited by Richard A. Niemi and Herbert F. Weisberg, pp. 332-57. Columbus, Ohio: Merrill.

Converse, Philip E., Aage Clausen, and Warren E. Miller. 1965. "Electoral Myth and Reality: The 1964 Election." American Political Science Review 59:321-33.

Crotty, William J. 1983. Party Reform. New York: Longman.

_____. 1977. Political Reform and the American Experiment. New York: Thomas Y. Crowell.

_____ and Gary C. Jacobson. 1980. American Parties in Decline. Boston: Little, Brown.

DeFelice, E. Gene. 1981. "Separating Professionalism from Pragmatism: A Research Note on the Study of Political Parties." American Journal of Political Science 25:796-807.

DiClerico, Robert E., and Eric M. Uslaner. 1984. Few Are Chosen: Problems in Presidential Selection. New York: McGraw-Hill.

Downs, Anthony. 1957. An Economic Theory of Democracy. New York: Harper and Row.

Edinger, Lewis J., and Donald D. Searing. 1967. "Social Background and Elite Analysis." American Political Science Review 61:428-45.

Edwards, Ward. 1968. "Decision Making: Psychological Aspects." International Encyclopedia of the Social Sciences, pp. 34-41. New York: MacMillan and the Free Press.

Farah, Barbara G., M. Kent Jennings, and Warren E. Miller. 1981. "Convention Delegates: Reform and the Representation of Party Elites, 1972-1980." Paper presented to the Conference on Party Activists, Williamsburg, Virginia.

Gibson, James L., Cornelius P. Cotter, John F. Bibby, and Robert J. Hickshorn. 1983. "Assessing Party Organizational Strength." American Journal of Political Science 27:193-222.

Gillespie, Michael W. 1977. "Log-linear Techniques and the Regression Analysis of Dummy Dependent Variables." Sociological Methods and Research 6:103-22.

Hitlin, Robert A., and John S. Jackson III. 1977. "On Amateur and Professional Politicians." Journal of Politics 39:786-93.

Hofstetter, C. Richard. 1971. "The Amateur Politician: A Problem in Construct Validation." Midwest Journal of Political Science 15:31-56.

Jackson, John S. III, Barbara Leavitt Brown, and David Bositis. 1982. "Herbert McClosky and Friends Revisited: 1980 Democratic and Republican Party Elites Compared to the Mass Public." American Politics Quarterly 10:158-80.

Keech, William R., and Donald R. Matthews. 1976. The Party's Choice. Washington, D.C.: Brookings.

Kessel, John. 1980. Presidential Campaign Politics: Coalition Strategies and Citizen Response. Homewood, Illinois: Irwin-Dorsey.

Key, V. O., Jr. 1958. Politics, Parties, and Pressure Groups. New York: Crowell.

Kirkpatrick, Jeane. 1976. The New Presidential Elite. New York: Russell Sage and Twentieth Century Fund.

____. 1978. Dismantling the Parties. Washington, D.C.: American Enterprise Institute.

Ladd, Everett Carll, Jr., with Charles D. Hadley. 1978. Transformations of the American Party System. New York: Norton.

Lengle, James I. 1981. Representation and Presidential Primaries. Westport, Connecticut: Greenwood Press.

Marshall, Thomas R. 1981. Presidential Nominations in a Reform Age. New York: Praeger.

Matthews, Donald. 1954. The Social Background of Political Decision Makers. Garden City, New York: Doubleday.

____, ed. 1973. Perspectives on Presidential Selection. Washington, D.C.: Brookings.

McClosky, Herbert, Paul J. Hoffman, and Rosemary O'Hara. 1960. "Issue Conflict and Consensus among Party Leaders and Followers." American Political Science Review 54:406-27.

Montjoy, Robert S., William R. Shaffer, and Ronald E. Weber. 1980. "Policy Preferences of Party Elites and Masses: Conflict or Consensus?" American Politics Quarterly 8:319-44.

Nakamura, Robert T. 1980. "Beyond Purism and Professionalism: Styles of Convention Delegate Followership." American Journal of Political Science 24:207-32.

____, and Denis G. Sullivan. 1982. "Neo-Conservatism and Presidential Nomination Reforms: A Critique." Congress and the Presidency 9:

Page, Benjamin I. 1978. Choices and Echoes in Presidential Elections. Chicago: University of Chicago Press.

Polsby, Nelson W. 1983. Consequences of Party Reform. New York: Oxford University Press.

____, and Aaron Wildavsky. 1980. Presidential Elections: Strategies of American Electoral Politics. New York: Charles Scribner's.

Pomper, Gerald, et al. 1981. The Election of 1980. Chatham, New Jersey: Chatham House.

Putnam, Robert D. 1976. The Comparative Study of Political Elites. Englewood Cliffs, New Jersey: Prentice-Hall.

Ranney, Austin. 1975. Curing the Mischiefs of Faction: Party Reform in America. Berkeley: University of California Press.

____. 1977. Participation in American Presidential Nominations, 1976. Washington, D.C.: American Enterprise Institute.

Republican National Committee. 1982. Commonsense. Issue devoted to "The Conference on the Parties and the Nominating Process." Volume 5.

Roback, Thomas H. 1975. "Amateurs and Professionals: Delegates to the 1972 Republican National Convention." Journal of Politics 37:436-68.

____. 1980. "Motivation for Activism among Republican National Convention Delegates: Continuity and Change, 1972-1976." Journal of Politics 42:181-201.

Sorauf, Frank J. 1980. Party Politics in America, 4th ed. Boston: Little, Brown.

Soule, John W., and James W. Clarke. 1970. "Amateurs and Professionals: A Study of Delegates to the 1968 National Convention." American Political Science Review 64:888-98.

____. 1971. "Issue Conflict and Consensus: A Comparative Study of Democratic and Republican Conventions." Journal of Politics 33:65-76.

Soule, John W., and Wilma E. McGrath. 1975. "A Comparative Study of Presidential Nomination Conventions: The Democrats of 1968 and 1972." American Journal of Political Science 19: 501-19.

Stone, Walter J. 1984. "Prenomination Candidate Choice and General Election Behavior: Iowa Presidential Activists in 1980." American Journal of Political Science, in press.

____, and Alan I. Abramowitz. 1983. "Winning May Not Be Everything, But It's More Than We Thought: Presidential Party Activists in 1980." American Political Science Review 77:xxx-yyy.

Sullivan, Denis G. 1977-78. "Party Unity: Appearance and Reality." Political Science Quarterly 92:635-45.

____, Jeffrey L. Pressman, Benjamin I. Page, and John J. Lyons. 1974. The Politics of Representation: The Democratic Convention of 1972. New York: St. Martin's Press.

United States Department of Commerce. 1982. State and Metropolitan Area Data Book. Washington, D.C.: Government Printing Office.

Watson, Richard A. 1980. The Presidential Contest. New York: Wiley.

Wattenberg, Martin P. 1981. "The Decline of Political Partisanship in the United States: Negativity or Neutrality?" American Political Science Review 75:941-50.

Wayne, Stephen J. 1981. The Road to the White House: The Politics of Presidential Elections. New York: St. Martin's Press.

Wildavsky, Aaron. 1965. "The Goldwater Phenomenon: Purists, Politicians, and the Two-Party System." Review of Politics 17:386-413.

Wilson, James Q. 1962. The Amateur Democrat. Chicago: The University of Chicago Press.

INDEX

Miller, Warren E., 7, 81
Motivations of activists, see Incentives of activists

Nakamura, Robert T., 134
National Education Association, 41
Nixon, Richard, 135

O'Hara, Rosemary, 127
Ordeshook, Peter C., 7

Page, Benjamin I., 20, 73, 122
Partisanship among activists, 49, 55, 80
Party organizations, viability of, 8-10, 20-21, 22, 122, 125-27, 135-36
Political experience of activists, 49-51, 111, 117-21
Political style, see Purism vs. pragmatism
Polsby, Nelson W., 3, 5, 9, 10, 11, 24, 117, 126, 133, 136
Presidential party caucuses, v, 11, 13, 24, 135-36; in Iowa, 12, 15, 16; in Maine, 17; in North Dakota, 17; in South Carolina, 16, 17; in Virginia, 17
Presidential primaries, v-vi, 10-12, 13, 20, 24, 126, 135-36; in Massachusetts, 17; in New Hampshire, 13, 15, 16
Professional style, see Purism vs. pragmatism
Purism vs. pragmatism, 3-4, 5-6, 46, 47-48, 52, 54, 130; and candidate choice, 45, 51-54, 85-87, 111, 113, 117, 119, 131; and ideology, 51-52; and incentives, 48-

49; measurement of, 46; and political experience, 49-51, 130
Purist model, 2-3, 4-6, 10-11, 21-22, 23, 93, 95, 96, 99; and candidate choice, 17-20, 43-44, 46-54; and party organizations, 7-9, 20-21
Putnam, Robert D., 24

Ranney, Austin, 133
Rational choice model, see expected utility model
Reagan, Ronald: bases of support for, 19-20, 82-88, 93, 101, 105, 108-09, 113, 116, 131; 1976 campaign, 45; 1980 campaign, 14-19, 31-32, 52, 56; characteristics of supporters, 17, 19, 32-34, 40-43, 52-54, 62-70, 128, 130; electability of, 73-80, 131, 132; ideology of, 61, 129
Roback, Bruce, 3, 45, 46
Rohde, David W., 14

Searing, Donald D., 24
Social characteristics of activists: and candidate choice, 27-34, 43-44, 191; interparty differences, 23, 25-27, 43, 127-28; interstate differences, 27-29; and party reforms, 24-25, 126-27; and representation, 127
Sorauf, Frank J., 13
Soule, John W., 3, 6, 45, 46, 52, 85
Stokes, Donald E., 81
Stone, Walter J., 7, 133, 134
Sullivan, Denis G., 45

ABOUT THE AUTHORS

ALAN I. ABRAMOWITZ is Associate Professor of Political Science at the State University of New York at Stony Brook. He has published several articles in the areas of voting behavior, political parties, and legislative behavior. His articles have appeared in the American Political Science Review, the American Journal of Political Science, the Journal of Politics, the Western Political Quarterly, the International Political Science Review, and Political Behavior. Dr. Abramowitz holds a B.A. from the University of Rochester and a Ph.D. from Stanford University.

WALTER J. STONE is Associate Professor of Political Science at the University of Colorado. His research interests in American politics include the political parties, presidential nominations, congressional representation, and voting behavior. He has published his work on these topics in such journals as the American Journal of Political Science, American Political Science Review, American Politics Quarterly, British Journal of Political Science, Western Political Quarterly, and others. He received his B.A. degree from the University of San Francisco, an M.A. from the University of Colorado, and a Ph.D. from the University of Michigan.